Savannah
CELEBRATIONS
Simple Southern Party Menus

Martha Nesbit

Photography by
Erin Adams

Styling by
Elizabeth Demos

PELICAN PUBLISHING COMPANY
Gretna 2010

This book is a collaborative effort. Photographer Erin Adams made the food look mouth-watering, stylist Elizabeth Demos made the parties come alive, and designer/packager Janice Shay whipped us all into shape and made the book flow. Thank you, ladies!
Thanks additionally to the homeowners who allowed us to showcase their homes and settings—Sidney and Colleen Smith, Steve and Polly Stramm, Eddie and Cynthia DeLoach, Carey and Ginger Shore, and Patrick Shay.
To my cooking friends who shared recipes, I love you!

The word "Pelican" and the depiction of a pelican are trademarks of Pelican Publishing Company, Inc., and are registered in the U.S. Patent and Trademark Office.

ISBN-13: 978-1-58980-835-5

Printed in China

Published by Pelican Publishing Company, Inc.
1000 Burmaster Street, Gretna, Louisiana 70053

To my men—Gary, Zack, and Emory, who make me want to cook

And

*To my mother, Alice Jo, who **really** wanted me to do this cookbook*

Contents

Introduction

This collection of recipes is the result of more than thirty years of inviting people into my Savannah home for casual suppers, baby showers, special birthday dinners, and meals prepared for bridge friends, prom couples, and fraternity boys on their way home from a beach weekend. This book is about how to prepare a Low Country boil for your family, or for forty, which we do each year for the Giddens clan down at the River House at Shellman Bluff in McIntosh County. It's about how to use up the fish that a neighbor caught off-shore fishing. It's about how to make a crab cake and how to fry a corn pone. It's about how to plan for the holidays—Thanksgiving, Christmas, St. Patrick's Day and the Fourth of July. It's about transforming dinner into a wonderful occasion for you, your family and guests, whether it's a special event or just the celebration of vine-ripe summer tomatoes or fresh corn on the cob that you picked that day or discovered at the local farmers' market.

The theme of this cookbook is simple recipes with a Southern feel, served casually in spectacular settings—on a weathered side porch at Tybee Island, upon a picnic quilt thrown on the sand at the beach, from a kitchen countertop buffet, or the back of a pick up for a game-day tailgate party.

The parties are set against a variety of beautiful backdrops full of romantic details—wrought iron, historic Savannah gray brick townhomes, live oaks dripping with moss, marsh grass swaying in the breeze, palmetto fronds, wooden dock houses overlooking the Intracoastal waterway, walled gardens, sand dunes and sea oats on Tybee beach, downtown squares, and two-hundred-year-old mansions. For all these reasons, travel writers consider Savannah one of the most beautiful cities in the world, and I agree!

I have been writing about Southern food, Savannah-style, for thirty-five years, since I graduated from Georgia Southern College (now a university) in Statesboro, Georgia, with a bachelor's of science degree in Home Economics. I spent eleven years as the food editor of the *Savannah Morning News*, reviewed restaurants for the newspaper as a freelancer for another seven years, and since 1998 have been a columnist for *Savannah Magazine* and an occasional caterer. In addition, I have written or participated in the writing of ten cookbooks, including a few with my friend Paula Deen—*Paula Deen and Friends, Paula Deen Celebrates, My First Cookbook,* and *Paula Deen's Cookbook for the Lunch-Box Set.* I cherish our friendship and so appreciate what Paula has done to market our beautiful city.

Like all cooks, I've was influenced by the food cooked for me as a child by my mother, Alice Jo Giddens of Valdosta, Georgia, my grandmother, the late Mary Lane of Statesboro, my aunt, the late Sue Lane of Statesboro, and my Aunt Betty Lane of Statesboro, as well as the wonderful new Northern dishes I picked up from my mother-in-law, Mona Nesbit. I am also lucky to have friends who are terrific cooks and who didn't mind sharing a secret recipe or two. Being generous is a Southern thing.

As a young food editor, I was privileged to attend cooking demonstrations given by some of the world's top chefs—Abby Mandel taught me to use a new-

fangled kitchen device called the Cuisinart 30 years ago; Wolfgang Puck taught food editors to make colored pasta; and PBS food commentator Vertamae Grosvernor demonstrated the fine art of making shrimp perlou. Memories I will always cherish include riding in an elevator with the delightful Julia Child and dancing a waltz with Craig Claiborne! Years later, Food Network star Bobby Flay came to my Isle of Hope kitchen for a morning to film a "Food Nation With Bobby Flay" segment; he featured my shrimp and grits in his cookbook "Bobby Flay Cooks American" and added his version to the menu of the Mesa Grill in New York. I have always thought that people who love food and love to cook food for others are truly the nicest people.

So, Martha, why a menu cookbook, you ask? I really want to inspire a new generation of cooks to invite people into their homes. This book is about how to put together a small home party and either buy the food or cook it yourself without a caterer (apologies to my catering buddies.) It's about having guests wonder how you pulled it off with such ease. It's about having everyone asking for your recipes, and calling you for your menu ideas!

When planning a party, many readers through the years have said that the most difficult part is deciding on the menu, so this book includes my suggestions about what goes with what. Certain food combinations really do taste better than others. This book is also about thinking through your work plan so that all the food is ready on time so that you've got time to shower and brush your teeth before the guests arrive. Successful parties really don't "just happen." Instead of enjoying the company, I was caught cooking at several of my early attempts at party-giving. On several occasions, my main course was served at 10 p.m. instead of 7. And yes, I cooked the package of giblets in my first turkey. However, now I know better, and I want you to know better, too.

Because of my home economics background, I am a cook who is always mindful of safety in the kitchen. I am always thinking of time-saving innovations, and always considering how the food will look on the plate with regards to color and texture. When possible, I like for my food to be healthy, although celebrations are not the best time to diet and watch your salt and fat intake. And yes, Mother, I'm thrifty, too, although I do splurge on shrimp and filet mignon.

In 1998, I became interested in education, returning to GSU to become certified to teach. Then, I earned a master's degree in education from Armstrong Atlantic State University, and became director of instruction at Oglethorpe Charter School, the public middle school which I was instrumental in founding. I come from a long line of educators—my mother, aunt and grandmother were all teachers—and so it is no accident that I enjoy teaching others how to solve an equation, write an essay, and how to cook. I hope these recipes provide you with the detailed instructions you will need so that your dishes turn out perfectly.

Cooking has provided me with so much pleasure, and I hope you will learn to love it as I do. Friends and readers have told me they like my recipes because they are simple, don't call for exotic ingredients, and taste delicious. I hope that's what you find in this collection, and that your parties will give you the warm memories that mine have provided me.

Let's eat!

Christening Party

Anything that has to do with babies is a good thing. But typically, the poor parents who had the baby are also hosting the party, and they find themselves frazzled beyond belief. *Will the baby cry? Will the baby .... on the christening gown? Will the in-laws get along? How does my dress hang in the back? Will the minister drop the baby?* (I know I shouldn't even think that!)

My point is: The menu better be easy, easy, easy! This is a time to call in friends and family to pitch in. Let the grandmothers fight over the baby, put your brother-in-law in charge of the drink table, ask your favorite aunt to man the oven, have a runner to make sure platters are refilled, and, if you can afford it, pay someone to stand in the kitchen and keep everything washed up so that, when the guests leave, your entire household can nap.

The work plan is easy—prepare EVERYTHING in advance and have it covered in the refrigerator, with sticky notes on top telling how long it

is to be baked and at what temperature. Just before leaving for the church, remove everything from the refrigerator so it will not be stone cold. That way, the ham rolls and quiche will bake in twenty minutes, while your guests are oohing and aahing over everything that happened during the service. Have all of the serving platters out, let your kitchen helper plate the food, and let your guests serve themselves. The aroma coming from your oven will have all your guests salivating, which adds to the success of any party.

Tips

Prepare all the food in advance and put sticky notes on top of each dish telling how long the food is to be baked and at what temperature.

Remember to appoint a photographer to document the day.

Lay everything out several days in advance so you will see what is missing.

Specifically appoint the following helpers:

   baby-handler
   drink-maker
   oven-helper
   runner
   photographer
   dish washer

A bowl of fresh fruit or a vegetable tray would add color and crunch to this menu. I recommend purchasing these from the produce section of a good grocery store, or assigning a friend to bring.

Mint Juleps Serves 12

A mint julep is best in the spring and summer, but it's a fine drink any season. Everyone has a different idea of what qualifies as a "real" mint julep, but I've never had anyone complain about these.

1 bottle Kentucky bourbon
Crushed ice
Mint sprigs for garnish

Mint Syrup (makes 1 1/2 cups):
1 cup sugar
1 cup water
2 cups lightly packed fresh mint

To make the mint syrup, combine sugar and water in a saucepan. Bring to a boil, stirring gently to dissolve, then boil 5 minutes without stirring. Remove from heat, add mint and cover saucepan. Let sit until cool. Strain into jar. Keep refrigerated until ready to use. Makes about 1 1/2 cups.

For each drink, fill tall glass with crushed ice. Add 1 jigger mint syrup and 1 1/2 jiggers bourbon. Stir. Add more ice if necessary. Garnish with sprig of mint.

Mimosas Serves 12

This is a beautiful, celebratory drink.

1 bottle Champagne, chilled
2 quarts orange juice, chilled
Fresh mint

Fill each champagne or wine glass half full with orange juice, then add champagne. Garnish with fresh mint sprigs.

Tomato Pie   Serves 8

Someone brought me this pie when one of my babies was hospitalized many years ago, and I've treasured the recipe ever since! Allow it to rest about 10 minutes before cutting so that the slices will be prettier. It's delicious even when the tomatoes are not at their best.

1 (9-inch) pie shell, cooked and cooled	4 ounces Cheddar cheese
2 tablespoons Dijon mustard	4 ounces Swiss cheese
4 peeled, sliced tomatoes, drained on paper towels	2 tablespoons mayonnaise
Salt and pepper to taste	3 tablespoons Parmesan cheese

When pie shell is cool, spread Dijon mustard on shell. Layer sliced tomatoes, salt, pepper, and cheeses, ending with cheese. For top layer, spread mayonnaise over cheese (this is hard to do, but it will spread evenly during cooking). Sprinkle with Parmesan cheese.

Preheat oven to 350 degrees F. Bake pie until bubbly, about 20 minutes. Allow to sit for about 10 minutes before cutting. Cut into 8 wedges.

Challah

This bread is a standard at Savannah's Jewish celebrations and it happens to be my son's favorite. It's sweet, yeasty, and delicious with soft butter. You might not think you need it for this menu, but the kids will love you for it. Leftover slices make wonderful French toast.

1 tablespoon dry yeast
1/4 cup warm water (105 to
   115 degrees F)
1/2 cup milk
1/2 cup butter or margarine, at
   room temperature

1/3 cup sugar, plus 1 tablespoon
1/2 teaspoon salt
3 1/4 cups all-purpose flour
3 beaten eggs
1 beaten egg yolk (reserve white for
   glazing bread)

Soften yeast in warm water. Heat milk; cool to lukewarm. In heavy-duty mixer, or by hand, thoroughly cream butter, 1/3 cup sugar and salt. Add milk and 1 cup of flour. Mix well. Add yeast, 3 eggs, and extra yolk, beating well between each egg. Add remaining flour. Beat 5 to 8 minutes longer. (Dough will be soft.)

Cover with lightweight kitchen towel and allow to rise in warm spot until doubled in bulk, about 2 hours. Stir down with a wooden spoon, mixing well. Place in a very large sealed container and allow to rise in the refrigerator overnight.

Punch dough down with your fist and turn out on slightly floured surface. Divide the dough into 3 pieces and roll each into a long piece. Braid the 3 pieces together and place on greased baking sheet. Cover; let rise until double. Brush the top of the bread with reserved egg white beaten with 1 tablespoon sugar.

Bake at 350 degrees F for 25 or 30 minutes, or until done.

Note: This bread freezes beautifully in a resealable plastic bag. When ready to serve, allow the bread to come to room temperature, then place it in hot oven for 5 minutes. Microwaving is not recommended for crusty breads.

Vidalia Onion Quiche   Serves 8

This recipe ran in my column in Savannah Magazine, *and it keeps cropping up at covered-dish events throughout Savannah. I recommend pre-cooking it and then reheating the day of the christening party.*

---

4 slices bacon, minced

1 large Vidalia onion, chopped

3 tablespoons flour

2 cups half-and-half

3 eggs

1/2 teaspoon salt

1/4 teaspoon pepper

1/2 teaspoon dried thyme

1 ready-to-roll pie crust

1/2 cup shredded Swiss cheese

1/2 cup grated Parmesan cheese

Preheat oven to 425 degrees F.

Fry the bacon in a medium skillet until it is very crisp. Remove the bacon to a paper towel to drain. Drain off all but one tablespoon of the bacon grease. Sauté the onion in the grease until it is very tender and just beginning to turn brown, about 10 to 12 minutes. Stir in the flour.

In a quart measuring cup, measure the half-and-half. Add the eggs and whisk together. Add the salt, pepper, and thyme. Place the pie crust in a deep-dish glass pie dish. Crimp the edges. Prick the bottom and sides of the crust. Layer both cheeses in the bottom of the crust. Distribute the bacon pieces and sautéed onion over the cheese. Pour the egg mixture over all.

Place the pie dish on a cookie sheet for ease in handling and put in the center of heated oven. Bake for 10 minutes at 425 degrees F, then reduce the temperature to 350 degrees F and bake for 45 minutes longer, or until the center of the quiche is set. You may need to cover the outer edge of the crust with foil to prevent over-browning.

Cool, then cover and refrigerate. The day of the party, place the quiche in a warm oven (300 degrees F) for about 15 minutes.

Hot Ham and Cheese Rolls Serves 8 to 10

This recipe is a perfect accompaniment to the rest of the menu items and, and can be made up ahead of time.

3 (7 1/2 -ounce) packages party rolls in
   aluminum trays
1 cup butter or margarine, melted
3 tablespoons prepared mustard
4 tablespoons poppy seed

1 medium onion, finely chopped
1 teaspoon Worcestershire sauce
1 pound of premium deli sliced ham
1 pound Swiss cheese slices

Combine butter, mustard, poppy seed, onion, and Worcestershire sauce. Slice rolls in half horizontally with a long bread knife, without separating rolls. Spread both sides of rolls with butter mixture. Layer ham and cheese; replace top of rolls. Wrap in foil and refrigerate.

   Preheat oven to 400 degrees F. Bake rolls, covered, for 15 minutes.

··

Apple Cheese Casserole Serves 4 to 6

This recipe is not only perfect for brunch, but is also delicious with any menu featuring pork.

1/2 cup softened butter
1 cup sugar
8 ounces sharp Cheddar cheese,
   grated
3/4 cup all-purpose flour

1-pound can sliced apples,
   unsweetened, or 6 Granny Smith
   apples, peeled, diced and stewed in
   1/2 cup water for 15 minutes

Preheat oven to 325 degrees F. Cream butter and sugar in a medium mixing bowl. Add cheese and stir with a spoon. Add flour and combine using fingers or a spoon. Batter will be stiff. Place apples in a 1 1/2 -quart casserole sprayed with vegetable spray. Evenly crumble cheese mixture over apples. Bake for 30 minutes.

Chocolate Surprise Bars Makes 32 bars

This recipe has a shortbread crust, chocolate layer, and is polished off with a layer that tastes like pecan pie. What's not to love? These also make a great hostess gift.

First Layer:
1/2 cup butter, at room temperature

1 egg yolk

2 tablespoons water

1 1/4 cups all-purpose flour

1 teaspoon sugar

1 teaspoon baking powder

1/8 teaspoon salt

Second Layer:
1 (12-ounce) package semi-sweet
   chocolate chips

Third Layer:
2 eggs

3/4 cups sugar

6 tablespoons melted butter

2 cups finely chopped pecans or
   walnuts

1 1/4 teaspoons vanilla extract

Confectioners' sugar (optional)

Preheat oven to 350 degrees F.

For first layer: In a mixing bowl, cream butter and beat in egg yolk and water. Mix well. Sift together flour, sugar, baking powder, and salt. Add to butter mixture. With floured hands, press into greased 13 x 9-inch pan. Bake about 10 minutes, or until lightly browned.

For second layer: Remove pan from oven and sprinkle chocolate chips evenly over crust. Return pan to oven until chips melt, about 2 minutes. Spread chocolate layer evenly over crust with a metal spatula.

For third layer: Beat eggs until thick in same mixing bowl you used for first layer. Beat in sugar. Stir in butter, nuts, and extract. Mix well. Pour evenly over chocolate layer.

Return to oven and bake 25 to 30 minutes, or until a light golden brown and dough springs back when touched. Cool completely in the pan. Cut into bars. Sprinkle with confectioners' sugar if desired.

Store in airtight container at room temperature. Note: Chocolate layer will begin to melt if bars get hot. Bars keep for several weeks in the refrigerator. They also freeze well.

Sis's Sugar Cookies   Makes 8 to 10 dozen

I don't know where the original recipe came from, but my mother's been making these crisp, huge sugar cookies for years now. Her grandchildren demand an ample supply for family vacations. They will keep your young guests occupied until the real food is ready.

4 cups unsifted all-purpose flour	1 cup confectioners' sugar
1 teaspoon salt	1 cup granulated sugar, plus more for
1 teaspoon baking soda	coating cookies
1 teaspoon cream of tartar	2 eggs
1 cup butter or margarine	1 teaspoon vanilla extract
1 cup vegetable oil	

In medium bowl, combine flour, salt, baking soda, and cream of tartar. In large mixer at medium speed, cream butter, oil, confectioners' sugar, and 1 cup granulated sugar until light and fluffy. Add eggs and vanilla and continue beating, scraping sides of bowl. Gradually add dry ingredients; mix until just combined. Wrap with plastic wrap and refrigerate dough for at least an hour.

Preheat oven to 350 degrees F.

Shape dough into 1-inch balls; roll in additional granulated sugar. Place on greased cookie sheets. Press each ball with a fork. Bake for 10 to 12 minutes. Remove and cool on wire racks.

•••

Microwave Pralines   Makes 15 to 18

1 pound light brown sugar	1 teaspoon vanilla
1 cup heavy whipping cream	1 cup pecans
2 tablespoons butter	

In a microwave-safe 2-quart bowl, mix brown sugar and cream. Cover tightly with plastic wrap with a slit cut in the center, and microwave on high for 13 minutes. Carefully uncover (watch for steam!) and add butter and vanilla. Add pecans and stir. Scoop with a small scoop onto parchment paper. Cool and eat.

Devil's Food Sandwich Cookies Makes 12

1 (18 1/2 -ounce) package devil's food cake mix	4 tablespoons (1/2 stick) butter, at room temperature
2 eggs	1 1/2 cups confectioners' sugar, sifted
1/3 cup vegetable oil	1/2 teaspoon vanilla extract
4 ounces cream cheese, softened	

Preheat oven to 350 degrees F. Line cookie sheets with parchment paper.

In a large mixing bowl, combine the cake mix, eggs, and oil with an electric beater, mixing well. The mixture will be very stiff.

Roll walnut-size balls of dough between your palms and place them about 2 inches apart on the cookie sheet. Flatten each cookie with your palm.

Bake for 9 to 10 minutes. Allow to sit on cookie sheet several minutes before moving to a wire rack to cool.

Meanwhile, in a medium mixing bowl, combine cream cheese, butter, and sugar to make the icing.

When cookies are completely cool, spread about 1 tablespoon of icing on the underside of one cookie and top with another cookie to make a sandwich. Continue until all cookies and icing are used.

Store in large resealable freezer bags in freezer or refrigerator. Recipe can be doubled.

Casual
Bridge Supper

I have been a member of the Isle of Hope Bridge Club for more than twenty years, during which time my friends and I have gone from being the mothers of small children to being mothers of the bride and groom. We have celebrated debuts, graduations, engagements, and promotions. We have cried over lost parents. But mostly, we have laughed together and eaten together, and played a little bridge.

Some time ago, we started having little suppers because it was really easier than preparing lots of hors d'oeuvres. We also have had a few bridge sleepovers that included simple suppers and tasty breakfasts the next morning, lots of fun chatter, and a few hands of bridge.

Here are some of my favorite main courses and desserts. A scoop of yummy casserole, a nice salad or green beans, and a roll are all that is needed to keep bridge players happy. A stunning dessert an hour or so after dinner, however, is mandatory.

The work plan is to have EVERYTHING done prior to the party so that you can play a hand or two yourself.

Chicken Tetrazzini Serves 8

In Savannah, this dish can usually be found in some form at most covered-dish functions. It also freezes beautifully, so can be made in advance.

1 (3-pound) chicken, cooked and
    boned, stock reserved, or 3 large
    chicken breasts
1 teaspoon salt
6 tablespoons butter or margarine,
    divided
4 tablespoons flour
1 1/2 cups half-and-half
1 1/2 cups chicken stock, reserved from
    cooking chicken

1/4 cup sherry
8 ounces mushrooms, sliced
2 green onions, sliced
1 clove garlic, pressed or minced
Salt and pepper to taste
8 ounces thin spaghetti noodles
1/2 cup grated Parmesan cheese

Simmer chicken in 4 cups water salted water in a large stock pot until very tender, about 45 minutes. If using breasts, boil for about 30 minutes. Remove 1 1/2 cups stock and reserve. Save remaining stock to cook spaghetti noodles in. Remove chicken meat and shred into bite-size pieces.

Make cream sauce by melting 4 tablespoons butter in a small skillet. Add flour and whisk until smooth. Add half-and-half and stock slowly, stirring between each addition. Stir in the sherry.

Allow to cook over low heat until thickened and smooth, about 5 minutes.

Meanwhile, sauté mushrooms, green onions and garlic in remaining 2 tablespoons butter.

Cook spaghetti in remaining 2 1/2 cups stock, adding more water if needed so noodles can boil freely. Drain spaghetti.

Combine cooked noodles, chopped chicken, sautéed vegetables and cream sauce. Place in buttered 13 x 9 inch casserole dish. Sprinkle with Parmesan cheese. Cover and refrigerate or freeze until ready to bake.

When ready to bake, allow casserole to sit out for 30 minutes to take the chill off. Preheat oven to 375 degrees F. Bake, uncovered, for 30 minutes, or until Parmesan is lightly browned.

Shrimp Curry with Rice Ring Serves 8

The apple gives the shrimp the sweetness and the curry gives it a little bite. The condiments are essential to the dish, not optional! Great Savannah cook, Liz Palles, taught me how to do the rice ring.

4 tablespoons butter

1 large yellow onion, chopped fine

1/2 cup (Fugi or Granny Smith) apple, finely chopped

1/2 cup celery, finely chopped

1 1/2 cups water

1 tablespoon curry powder

2 cups half-and-half

3 pounds shrimp, cleaned and deveined

Rice Ring:

4 cups cooked rice

Parsley, finely chopped

Toppings:

Grated coconut

Chutney, your favorite brand

Chopped almonds

Bacon, cooked crisp and crumbled

Pickle relish, your favorite brand

Sauté onion, apple, and celery in butter. When wilted, add water. Let simmer until apple and celery are tender and most of the liquid has evaporated. Stir in curry powder. Add half-and-half. Cook gently until cream is reduced to sauce consistency, about 5 to 8 minutes. Refrigerate.

When ready to serve, bring mixture to simmer and add shrimp. Simmer until shrimp are just pink. Do not overcook.

Serve curry with small bowls of grated coconut, chutney, chopped almonds, crumbled bacon, pickle relish, or other specialty relishes for toppings.

To make the rice ring: Prepare 4 cups cooked rice according to package directions. Spray a 2-quart ring mold with vegetable cooking spray. Immediately before serving buffet, sprinkle finely chopped parsley evenly into a ring mold. Press rice into the mold and unmold it immediately onto serving platter. Pour shrimp curry into middle of ring. Have additional curry in a gravy boat with ladle.

Shrimp and Grits   Serves 6

This recipe is good for brunch or casual suppers. The grits hold up well for about 30 minutes. The shrimp cooks in 10 minutes, so you could excuse yourself long enough to cook them and then call everyone for dinner, served from the stove top.

Bobby Flay visited my Isle of Hope kitchen, where I made this dish for him. He wrote in Bobby Flay Cooks American, *"If there is one dish that makes me want to march down Fifth Avenue waving the American flag, it's shrimp and grits. I'll always be grateful to Martha Nesbit of Savannah for introducing me to this Southern dish."*

4 cups water	2 teaspoons lemon juice
1 teaspoon salt	2 tablespoons chopped parsley
1/2 teaspoon pepper	2 tablespoons sliced green onions
1 cup stone-ground grits	2 large cloves garlic, minced
4 tablespoon butter	1/4 teaspoon Old Bay Seasoning
2 cups shredded sharp Cheddar cheese	Finely chopped parsley, for garnish
2 pounds shrimp, peeled and deveined	
4 slices bacon, chopped fine	

In a heavy-bottomed non-stick pot, bring water, salt, and pepper to a boil. Add grits and stir well with a whisk. Cover the pot, and lower heat to low and cook grits until they are smooth and creamy, about 20 minutes. Stir occasionally to keep them from sticking. When done, turn off the heat. Add the butter and the shredded cheese and stir. Cover to keep warm.

While grits are cooking, wash shrimp and pat dry. Fry the bacon in a large skillet until it is very crisp. Remove the bacon from the fat. Drain off all but 1 tablespoon of the bacon grease. Stir fry the shrimp in the bacon grease until it turns pink, about 3 minutes. Add the lemon juice, chopped parsley, sliced green onions, garlic, and Old Bay. Sauté for about 1 minute.

Serve grits directly from the pot—one-half cup of grits with one-half cup of shrimp with juice spooned over the top. Garnish with reserved bacon bits and parsley.

Shrimp Perlou   Serves 4

You can double this if you are serving more than four guests. In Low Country cookbooks, you will see "perlou" and "perlow"—both misspellings of the word "pilau," a rice dish cooked with meat or fish. The late Roy Courington made this often for his family, and he gave the recipe to his daughter, Dottie, who gave it to me.

6 slices bacon	2 cups chicken stock
1 small onion, finely chopped	1 pound shrimp, peeled and deveined
3 ribs celery, finely chopped	
1 red bell pepper, finely chopped	**Sauce:**
1 cup rice, uncooked	1/2 cup mayonnaise
1 teaspoon Worcestershire sauce	3 tablespoons lemon juice

Sauté bacon in a 2-quart saucepan with lid. Remove bacon. Sauté the vegetables in the bacon grease. Add the rice and stir to coat the rice with grease. Add the Worcestershire sauce and stock, reduce heat, cover pot, and cook over low heat for about 20 minutes, until rice absorbs liquid. Gently stir in shrimp and cook until they are done, about 5 to 7 minutes, stirring occasionally. Crumble bacon and add to shrimp and rice.

Combine mayonnaise and lemon juice and stir well—consistency should be about that of heavy cream. Pass sauce with the perlou.

Green Beans with Almonds   Serves 8

When I need a never-miss vegetable accompaniment, I turn to this recipe. Now that produce comes from all over, green beans are available year-round. You may also buy the tiny haricot vert, turning this into a gourmet dish.

2 pounds fresh green beans, washed
  and tips removed
1 teaspoon salt
1/2 teaspoon pepper
1/4 teaspoon garlic powder

1/4 cup butter or margarine
1 (2-ounce) package slivered almonds
1/2 teaspoon salt
Juice of one lemon

Using a 2-quart pot, cook beans in 2 cups of water seasoned with salt, pepper, and garlic powder. Bring to a rolling boil, then reduce heat to medium, cover pot, and taste beans every 3 minutes until they are done to your liking, 8 to 10 minutes. Drain and return to hot pot.

In small skillet, melt butter. Add almonds and toss. Cook until crisp and lightly browned. Almonds burn easily. Remove from heat. Add salt and lemon juice. Pour mixture over hot, cooked beans.

Beans may be refrigerated at this point. When ready to serve, heat them in a large microwave-safe bowl, covered, for 3 to 4 minutes.

Mandarin-Bleu Cheese Salad   Serves 8

2 hearts of Romaine
1 (8-ounce) can mandarin oranges,
  drained
2 ounces bleu cheese, crumbled

1/3 cup croutons
2/3 cup vinaigrette, or ginger dressing
1/2 cup toasted almonds, walnuts, or
  pecans, optional garnish

Chop Romaine and store in a plastic bag until ready to toss salad. In a large bowl, place the lettuce, oranges, bleu cheese and croutons. Toss with dressing just before serving.

Sherry Cream Cake   Serves 8

I first tasted this cake at Elizabeth on 37th Street restaurant. My cheater version calls for a purchased angel food cake.

---

1 (10-inch) angel food cake, torn into bite-sized pieces
1 envelope unflavored gelatin
½ cup water
5 large egg yolks
¾ cup sugar, separated
¾ cup dry sherry
2 cups whipped cream, separated
1 teaspoon vanilla

Toasted almond slivers and whole raspberries or strawberries, to garnish

Raspberry Puree:
1 (10-ounce) package frozen sweetened strawberries
1 (10-ounce) package frozen raspberries
Juice of 1 lemon

Dissolve gelatin in water. In a separate bowl, beat egg yolks and 1/2 cup sugar until light-colored. Add sherry. Cook egg mixture in double boiler over moderate heat until it thickens enough to coat the back of a metal spoon. Whisk the gelatin into the warm custard. Stir until completely dissolved.

Whip 1 cup of cream until thickened. Add vanilla. Combine custard and whipped cream. Fold cake pieces into custard cream until all are coated. Pour into a buttered 10-inch tube pan. Smooth with a spatula. Cover and refrigerate until set.

Unmold by wrapping pan with a warm towel for a few seconds, then turn out onto a plate. Ice cake with extra cup of whipped cream whipped until stiff with 1/4 cup sugar. Decorate with toasted almond slivers and whole raspberries.

Serve slices with raspberry puree. Garnish with extra toasted almond slivers, whole raspberries, or strawberries.

To make the raspberry puree: Place strawberries, raspberries, and lemon juice in a food processor and process until smooth. Strain for seeds (time-consuming but necessary). Keep covered in the refrigerator until ready serve. Also delicious on ice cream.

Irish Lace Cookies   Makes about 2 ½ dozen cookies

These are buttery, delicate, and delicious. The name may come from the Irish oatmeal used in the original recipes, or from the little holes that appear while the cookies are baking.

1/2 cup butter, at room temperature
3/4 cup sugar
1 egg
1 teaspoon vanilla

3 tablespoons all-purpose flour
1/2 teaspoon salt
1 cup quick-cooking oatmeal

Preheat oven to 350 degrees F. Cream butter and sugar. Add egg and vanilla and cream again. Add flour, salt, and oatmeal, mixing well with a rubber spatula. Drop by teaspoon onto foil-lined pans. Bake for 8 to 9 minutes, until lightly browned. Let cool before peeling from foil.

Cookies freeze well. Store in tins, as they crumble easily.

•••

Cheese Biscuits   Serves 8

These smell great and are easy as pie to make. If you have leftovers, split them, toast them, and top with strawberry jam or orange marmalade for breakfast.

3 cups self-rising flour
1 cup solid shortening
8 ounces sharp Cheddar cheese,
    grated

1 cup buttermilk

Preheat oven to 400 degrees F. Combine flour and shortening in food processor, or cut shortening into flour with two knives, scissor-fashion. Mix in cheese with your hands. Add buttermilk. Stir gently until ingredients are combined. Batter will be quite moist. Drop by tablespoon onto non-stick baking sheet. Bake for 10 minutes. Serve hot with softened butter.

Ladyfinger Truffle Mousse   Serves 8

This is for chocolate lovers. You can prepare this in one large dish, or individual dishes with la-dyfingers cut in half.

---

2 packages ladyfingers

Coffee syrup:
1/2 cup brewed coffee
3 tablespoons sugar
1/4 cup Kahlua or Amaretto

Mousse:
12 ounces semisweet chocolate chips
3 egg yolks, beaten well
1/4 cup brewed coffee

1 teaspoon vanilla extract
1/4 cup Kahlua or Amaretto
2 pints whipping cream, whipped (one
    for mousse and one for topping)
1/2 cup sliced almonds, toasted

Toppings:
Whipped cream
Chocolate shavings or chips
Fresh raspberries

Line a glass bowl with ladyfingers, placing some on the bottom of the bowl and standing as many as you can round the sides.

In a micro-waveable dish, combine coffee syrup ingredients. Heat in microwave about 1 minute, until hot enough to dissolve sugar. Stir well. Spoon syrup over ladyfingers until all is used.

Place chocolate chips in glass bowl. Microwave on high for 1 minute. Stir until chips are melted. Return to microwave and heat again for 1 minute, until quite hot. Quickly stir in egg yolks and whisk vigorously. (You want the eggs to get very hot to reduce the risk of salmonella.) Stir in coffee, vanilla extract, and Kahlua or Amaretto.

Whip 1 pint of cream until stiff. Stir into warm chocolate mixture. It will resemble chocolate pudding. Pour into center of bowl. It will come almost to the top of the ladyfingers.

Lightly toast sliced almonds (about 2 minutes in toaster oven). Sprinkle over top of the mousse.

Refrigerate for several hours or overnight. Mousse will become very firm. When ready to serve, spoon into small bowls and garnish with whipped cream, chocolate shavings, and fresh raspberries.

Salute to Gullah Cooking

Gullah refers to the combination of African and Low Country cultures. In the 1700s, Africans were brought to the coast to tend the rice fields, and they brought with them their culinary traditions, adapting them to the foods that were available along the coast—rice, seafood, corn, sweet potatoes, tomatoes, collards, turnips, peanuts, okra, eggplant, beans, and peas, often seasoned with whatever smoked meat that was leftover from hog-killings. The dishes that resulted are some of the most flavorful in the South.

Sesame seeds, also called benne seed, play a special role in Gullah cooking. Once, when I was a food writer for the *Savannah Morning News*, I interviewed public television food journalist Vertamae Grosvernor. I offended her greatly when I suggested that slaves might have brought benne seed to the new world in the pockets of their clothes. She reminded me that most of them were stripped naked, and there were no pockets in which to hide benne seeds. However, the seeds made their way from Africa to the United States during the slave years, and slaves often threw them near their front stoops for good luck. Slave cooks also threw them into one-pot dishes, such as the oyster pilau, for added taste and crunch. In this menu, they are baked into my favorite cookie, the benne seed wafer.

This is a meal to share with special friends who love the Low Country and appreciate its unique culinary history—a marriage of English, African, and coastal traditions. You'll note that several of the dishes are seasoned with pork—specifically bacon—and salt, pepper, and cayenne, Gullah's favorite trio. I can't think of a meal that warms the heart more than deviled crab, okra and tomatoes, turnips, corn pone, and sweet potato pie! No wonder such cooking is called soul food.

Oyster Perlou Serves 6 to 8

6 to 8 slices bacon

1 medium onion, chopped fine

1/2 cup chopped green pepper

1/2 cup chopped celery

1 1/4 cups raw rice

2 cups oyster liquid and chicken stock

1 pint oysters

In large frying pan, cook bacon until crisp. Crumble and set aside. Add onions, celery, and green pepper to bacon fat and cook until tender. Heat oysters in their liquid in saucepan until edges curl; remove oysters and reserve 2 cups of liquid. If there is not enough liquid, add enough chicken stock to make 2 cups.

Add rice, liquid, and oysters to vegetable mixture in frying pan. Bring to a rolling boil, stirring occasionally. Cover pot, lower heat, and continue to simmer until rice has absorbed liquid, about 15 minutes.

Okra and Tomatoes Serves 6 to 8

Whenever I fix this dish for Northerners they say, "I thought okra was slimy. It's delicious!" This is good made with frozen okra and canned tomatoes, too, if you can't get fresh.

4 slices hickory-smoked bacon

1 large onion chopped

1 pound fresh okra, ends trimmed and
   sliced into 1/2-inch pieces, or one
   (10-ounce) bag frozen chopped okra

5 ripe tomatoes, peeled and chopped,
   or 1 (28-ounce) can whole peeled
   tomatoes, chopped, with juice

Salt and cayenne pepper to taste

1/2 cup chicken broth

Sauté bacon until crisp. Remove bacon from skillet and crumble. Add onion to bacon grease and cook until soft, about 3 minutes. Add okra and sauté for a minute in bacon fat. Add tomatoes and seasonings. Reduce heat. Simmer until okra is tender, about 20 minutes. Add chicken broth if mixture becomes too thick. Add crumbled bacon immediately before serving.

Spicy Deviled Crab Makes 8 deviled crabs

1/2 cup Bloody Mary mix

4 tablespoons butter

8 saltines, finely crumbled

1/4 teaspoon dry mustard

1/2 teaspoon salt, if needed

1/8 teaspoon cayenne pepper

1/8 teaspoon black pepper

1 tablespoon Worcestershire sauce

1 additional tablespoon butter

2 tablespoons minced green onion

1 tablespoon minced red pepper

1 tablespoon minced celery

1 egg

1 pound white or claw crab meat, picked through twice for shells

8 aluminum foil crab shells

Topping:

4 tablespoons butter

Dry bread crumbs

Paprika or cayenne pepper

Heat Bloody Mary mix. Add butter and stir to melt. Add crumbled saltines and seasonings, except salt. In a small saucepan, sauté green onion, red pepper, and celery in 1 tablespoon butter until limp, about 2 minutes. Add to Bloody Mary mixture. Add egg, mixing well. Carefully add crab meat and stir gently to combine. Taste and add salt if needed. Pack in shells. Cover with bread crumbs lightly sautéed in butter.

Sprinkle cayenne pepper or paprika on top, depending on desired amount of spice/heat.

Bake at 350 degrees F for about 20 minutes, until heated through.

Or, wrap deviled crabs in plastic wrap and place in freezer bag. Can be frozen for up to six months. When ready to eat, bake frozen crabs at 350 degrees F for 40 minutes, until filling is hot and tops of deviled crab are brown.

One crab is a perfect first course. If serving as a main meal, allow two per person. Discard foil shells after using.

Turnip or Collard Greens Serves 6 to 8

I actually prefer collards over turnip greens. They used to be difficult to cook, as you had to get the sand out of the greens before you could prepare them. Now that they come triple-washed and striped from their large stems in the grocery store, cooking them is a breeze. Be prepared for them to come to the top of the pot when you first put them on to cook, then ten minutes later, you'll just have a quarter pot left when they "cook down."

2 pounds fresh turnip greens or collards
2 small ham hocks
2 cups water
1 teaspoon salt

2 tablespoons butter or margarine,
   optional

Strip leaves from stems. If using collards that have not been washed, wash thoroughly in several changes of water. Cut leaves into strips. Place strips in large heavy-bottomed saucepan. Add ham hocks, water, and salt. Cook at medium heat for several minutes, then reduce heat to low, cover, and cook for about 45 minutes, until tender. Remove ham hocks. Add any small pieces of lean meat that you can pick from the bones. Discard the bones. Shred greens with two knives, used scissor fashion. Taste and add more salt if necessary. There will be a small amount of liquid, which is called pot liquor. Serve it with the corn pone (see *page 44*). Add 2 tablespoons butter or margarine to greens before serving, if desired.

Corn Pone Makes about 10 "pones"

I grew up eating these, probably because the recipe was easy for my mother to throw together quickly and didn't require the ingredients that corn bread does. My husband loves corn pones hot with soft butter.

1 1/2 cups stone-ground yellow corn meal	1 teaspoon salt
1 1/2 cups cold water	Vegetable oil for frying

In a bowl, stir together corn meal, cold water, and salt. Allow to sit for about 10 minutes. Mixture will thicken as it sits. Cover bottom of a large, flat-bottomed skillet with vegetable oil, about 3 tablespoons. When oil is hot, drop corn meal batter into oil by tablespoonfuls, spreading into 3-inch circles. Fry until brown on both sides, about 3-5 minutes per side.

Sweet Potato Pie Serves 8

If you like pumpkin pie, you'll love sweet potato pie, especially if you start with sweet potatoes that you bake yourself. Serve with whipped cream and a sprinkling of cinnamon.

1 (9-inch) deep-dish pie crust	3 eggs
1 1/4 cups sweet potatoes (2 medium sweet potatoes, punctured with a fork, and baked for about a hour), mashed, strings removed	3/4 cup evaporated milk
	1/2 teaspoon salt
	1/4 teaspoon freshly grated nutmeg
	1/4 teaspoon ground cloves
4 tablespoons butter	1/2 teaspoon ground cinnamon
3/4 cup light brown sugar	1/4 cup bourbon or dark rum

Preheat oven to 375 degrees F. Cream butter and sugar. Add the mashed sweet potatoes. Add eggs and milk. Beat well. Add seasonings and bourbon or rum. Pour filling into pie crust and bake in the center of oven for 40 minutes, until top is golden and center is set.

Mrs. Sullivan's Benne Wafers Makes about 12 dozen

Mrs. Sullivan is the late Sally Sullivan, a lifetime Savannah caterer who never learned to drive and who frequently invited me and my husband-to-be into her downtown dining room to enjoy her wonderful cooking. She gave me this treasured recipe.

1 pound light brown sugar	1 teaspoon baking powder
1 1/2 cups (3 sticks) butter	1/2 teaspoon salt
2 eggs	1 1/2 teaspoons vanilla
2 cups all-purpose flour	1 1/2 cups toasted sesame seeds

To toast sesame seeds: Place seeds in single layer on cookie sheet. Place in 350-degree F oven for about 5 minutes, watching carefully. They should just begin to lightly brown.

Preheat oven to 300 degrees F. Cream first three ingredients in a large mixing bowl. Sift flour, baking powder, and salt. Add to butter mixture. Stir until combined. Add vanilla. Stir in sesame seeds, mixing well. Drop by ½ teaspoonfuls onto parchment-lined paper on cookie sheets. Cook 16 to 18 minutes, until very brown. Note: Let cool completely on parchment, then lift off.

May be stored in airtight container for several weeks. Wafers also freeze well.

Tailgate
Party

Potential students to the University of Georgia are given a student-led tour, complete with a lesson on one of the most fundamental requirements of being a part of the Bulldog Nation: The UGA Cheer: *GOOOOOOOOO DAWGS......SIC 'EM... WOOF, WOOF, WOOF.* I know this because my son, Emory, is a Bulldog, and my husband and I had the privilege of watching a thousand or so young people practice the cheer during an orientation weekend. Oh, the Southern Pride. Of course, your team might be the Savannah State University Tigers, or the Georgia Tech Yellow Jackets, or the Georgia Southern Eagles, or even, heaven forbid, a team from another state. Whatever the team, it's important to eat well before and/or after watching the game. You may also find these recipes helpful for an inside game party.

This menu is unlike any other in the book because the dishes have to travel well. There are so many adorable containers with snap-on lids (that you are sure to be able to find in your team colors) to keep the dips and spreads from spilling on the car seats and floor mats. Be sure to keep cold foods cold, and it's up to you to find a way to heat the baked beans and grill the hot dogs—a small portable grill or crock pot with extension cord, etc.

Tips

Other items that will make your party more pleasurable:

A foldable table

Comfortable folding chairs, with pockets for drinks

Wet cloth in a plastic bag for spills

Hand sanitizer

Umbrellas

Bug spray, unfortunately

Chipped Beef Spread   Serves 8 to 10

Don't take this to your tailgate unless you've got a plan for some way to heat the dip, which makes it runny and delicious. I've included it for home sports parties. This recipe is as old as the hills, but men love it.

1 (8-ounce) package softened cream
  cheese
2 1/2 ounces dried beef, shredded
1/4 cup finely chopped green pepper
1/4 cup finely chopped red pepper

1 medium onion, finely chopped
1/2 teaspoon black pepper
1/2 cup sour cream
3/4 cup chopped pecans

Mix cream cheese well with dried beef, green and red peppers, onion, and black pepper. Fold in sour cream. Spoon into a small casserole dish. Top with pecans.

Bake at 350 degrees F for 20 minutes. Serve with crackers.

Fried Chicken Serves 4

You can get up early and fry your own chicken. Or, you can purchase chicken from your favorite frying establishment and eat it warm or keep it chilled and serve it cold. On game days, I can tell you from a nose-witness account that the aroma of chicken frying starts early in the morning in Athens, Georgia.

There is no one way to fry a chicken. My mother, Alice Jo, had her own ritual. She'd stand at the kitchen sink, water running, and with a few quick strokes with a sharp knife cut the chicken up just the way we children liked it—with a breast, two side breasts, and a pully bone. We all fought over the pully bone. Then she'd throw the pieces into a brown paper sack filled with seasoned flour (plenty of salt and pepper) and she'd shake it vigorously. When the grease (vegetable oil) was good and hot, she'd hand-deliver the pieces into the deep, heavy frying pan she preferred. (Back then, we'd reuse the grease several times and it was always a big deal when we had fried chicken made with "new" oil). She'd place the lid on the fryer for about 10 minutes. Then she'd turn the chicken to the other side and keep the lid off so the crust could crisp up, another ten minutes. She made a point of cooking the pieces with larger bones—legs and short thighs— longer than the others. She'd drain the chicken on a brown paper sack torn open so it would lay flat. We children always got the white meat, as well as the gizzard, liver, and heart, which we thought was an honor. Mother would have to eat the back and dark meat. She swore she loved it. That's the way mothers are.

---

1 fryer chicken, cut into pieces
Flour
Salt and pepper
Vegetable oil, about 3 cups

Early in the day, season chicken. Refrigerate in a casserole dish covered with plastic wrap. When ready to fry, toss chicken in bag with flour.

Heat oil in large skillet with lid. When hot, add chicken to hot oil one piece at a time. Do not crowd skillet. Cover and cook on medium high for about 10 minutes. Remove cover, turn chicken to other side and continue cooking on medium high for about 10 more minutes. Remove smaller pieces first. Drain on brown paper bags (or paper towels).

Chutney Cheese Ball   serves 8 to 10

I got stuck sitting next to a Chutney Cheese Ball one night at a party, and wound up eating the whole thing. I have never had a better time.

1 (8-ounce) package cream cheese, softened

1 teaspoon curry powder

1 teaspoon dry mustard

1 (9-ounce) bottle Major Grey's Chutney, divided

1/2 cup chopped pecans

1/2 cup shredded coconut

Blend all ingredients except coconut, using half of chutney. Add nuts last. Line a small glass bowl with plastic wrap, leaving lots of overhang. Using a spatula, pack the cream cheese mixture firmly into the bottom of the dish. Use the overhang to cover the top of the cream cheese. When firm, unwrap the top, invert the dish into your carrying dish, and snap on the lid. Keep chilled. When ready to serve, cover with rest of chutney and shredded coconut.

Serve with any bland cracker.

Mexican Dip Serves 8 to 10

I've never served this dish that I didn't get a call afterwards requesting the recipe. I've seen a dozen Mexican dip recipes, but this is the easiest, prettiest and best.

1 (1-pound) can refried beans
1 package taco seasoning mix
1 1/2 cups sour cream
2 tomatoes, diced
4 green onions, white and green parts,
  finely sliced
8 ounces grated cheddar cheese
Black olives for garnish, if desired
Corn chips, purchased or homemade

Guacamole (optional):
1 ripe avocado
Lemon juice
2 tablespoons sour cream
1/4 teaspoon garlic powder
1/4 teaspoon salt

Spread beans with a spatula in the bottom of a 13 x 9 inch plastic casserole dish with snap-on lid. In a small bowl, combine taco mix with sour cream. Cover beans with sour cream mixture. Layer tomatoes and green onions. Cover with guacamole, if using. Cover entire casserole with layer of cheese. Garnish with black olives, if desired, cut in half and placed in design on top of cheese.

Chill, covered, in container until ready to serve. Serve with chips.

Note: It is important that layers be thin, so do not prepare in a smaller pan. Halve recipe, instead.

To make guacamole: Mash avocado with lemon juice, sour cream, garlic powder, and salt.

Dottie's Baked Beans   Serves 12 to 14

Many people take a grill with them to the tailgate, and grill up a few hot dogs to serve along with everything else. I never like hotdogs unless they are cooked on the grill. Take along a small pot with a lid, and heat the beans while the dogs are grilling. With half a pound of bacon and two cups of brown sugar, how could these baked beans be anything but delicious? They are absolutely perfect for any covered dish supper or barbecue.

1/2 pound bacon, chopped into 1/2 inch
   pieces
2 large onions, chopped
1 (48-ounce) can pork and beans
2 cups dark brown sugar
1 cup ketchup
1/4 cup prepared mustard
1/4 cup Worcestershire sauce
2 teaspoons liquid smoke

In large Dutch oven, fry bacon until crisp. Remove bacon and all but 2 tablespoons of the grease. In bacon grease, fry onions until they are tender and transparent. To onions, add crumbled bacon, beans, sugar, ketchup, mustard, Worcestershire, and liquid smoke. Cook on low several hours, stirring occasionally.

Old Fashioned Potato Salad Serves 8 to 10

This is the traditional potato salad that I prefer above all others. I like it best with new potatoes, with the skins left on, but it's also good with baking potatoes.

4 baking potatoes, peeled and diced, or 8-12 new potatoes, cubed, with skin, left on
2 ribs of celery, diced
1/2 of a green pepper, diced
1/4 cup sweet salad cube pickles (not sour pickle relish)

1 1/2 teaspoons salt
1/4 teaspoon pepper
1 teaspoon prepared mustard, preferably Dijon
1 cup Hellman's mayonnaise
4 hard-cooked eggs, chopped

In a large stock pot, cook potatoes in salted water until tender. Drain. Place potatoes, celery, green pepper, and pickles in a bowl. Combine salt, pepper, mustard, and mayonnaise. Toss dressing with potatoes. Add chopped eggs, then toss lightly. Serve immediately, or chill before serving.

Chewy Chocolate Cookies Makes 18 big cookies

Gottlieb's was a famous Savannah baker, known for its breads, its cakes, its pies, and especially for its wonderful chocolate chewy meringue cookies. This is my version of the famous cookie.

2 cups confectioners' sugar

3 tablespoons powdered cocoa, sifted

1/4 teaspoon salt

1/4 cup all-purpose flour, sifted

3 egg whites

1 cup chopped pecans

Preheat oven to 350 degrees F. Stir together sugar, cocoa, salt, and flour. Add egg whites one at a time and beat well. When well-beaten, stir in chopped pecans.

Drop by tablespoonfuls onto parchment-lined baking sheets that have been sprayed with vegetable cooking spray. Bake for 12 to 13 minutes. Allow to sit on the parchment for about five minutes before moving with a spatula. Cool on waxed paper. Store in airtight container.

Best eaten the same day they are made.

Chocolate Bark Serves 8 to 10

This recipe shows up at oyster roasts, tailgates, and swim meets—anywhere that this tasty combination of toffee and chocolate might come in handy. It can be made with graham crackers instead of Saltines, but I prefer the Saltines.

1 sleeve of Saltine crackers, or more

1 cup butter or margarine

1 packed cup light-brown sugar

1 (12-ounce) package semi-sweet
  chocolate morsels

Preheat oven to 400 degrees F. Line a large cookie sheet with foil. Lay crackers on foil in a solid cover, crackers touching. Cover all the foil. If your pan is large, you may need more than one sleeve of crackers.

In a medium saucepan, boil butter and brown sugar for 3 minutes, stirring constantly. Pour over crackers, spreading to cover them all.

Bake for 5 to 7 minutes; do not allow sugar mixture to burn.

Remove from oven and allow to sit undisturbed about 3 minutes. Sprinkle chocolate chips evenly over candy and spread with a spatula as chocolate begins to melt.

Refrigerate. Chocolate will harden in about 30 minutes to an hour and candy can be broken into pieces. If weather is hot enough to melt chocolate, keep chilled until ready to serve.

Slice and Bake Oatmeal Cookies Makes 8 dozen

My mother-in-law, Mona Nesbit, makes wonderful cookies. These are her best oatmeals. They travel very well.

1 cup vegetable shortening	1 1/2 cups all-purpose flour
1/2 cup dark brown sugar	1 teaspoon salt
1/2 cup light brown sugar	1 teaspoon baking soda
1 cup granulated sugar	3 cups oatmeal
2 eggs, beaten	1/2 cup chopped pecans, toasted
1/2 teaspoon vanilla	

In a large mixing bowl, cream shortening and sugars.

In a separate bowl, mix eggs and vanilla together; then add sugar to mixture. Mix well.

Sift together flour, salt, and soda. Add to sugar mixture, mixing with spoon. Add oatmeal and nuts. Stir until mixed. Form dough into long rolls. Wrap in waxed paper. Chill.

When ready to bake, preheat oven to 375 degrees F.

Slice dough into 1/4 inch slices. Bake on ungreased cookie sheet at 375 degrees F or 10 to 13 minutes. Cool for one minute before transferring to wire racks to cool. Store in plastic freezer bags.

Cookies freeze well.

Birthday Dinner

When I was a little girl, my birthday night was the best day of the year, a time when I was allowed to choose my favorite menu— usually a roast cooked with a little pink in the center, white rice, canned beans, and poundcake for dessert. Well, my tastes have changed.

At our house of mostly males, birthdays come in two varieties—the meat birthday, or the seafood birthday. So, I provided those two options for you. This is a family birthday when you might invite an aunt or uncle or perhaps a best friend or significant other. If you want more people involved, perhaps you should look to the Low Country Boil or the Oyster Roast menus, which lend themselves to crowds.

The rum punch, shrimp paste, sour cream biscuits, and coconut pound cake go with either meal. Then, you either go with the items listed on the seafood menu, or the beef menu, depending on the wishes of the honoree.

Seafood-lover's Birthday Party

Prepare the Shrimp Paste, Coconut Cake, and Crab Cakes one day in advance. Refrigerate crab cakes on a baking sheet covered tightly with plastic wrap. You can freeze the crab cakes, wrapping individually with plastic wrap and then placing them all in a freezer bag. Thaw one day before you are going to cook the crab cakes.

The morning of the party, prepare the Red Rice up until the baking stage. Chop all of the vegetables for the vegetable stir fry and place them in small plastic bags. Have the biscuit ingredients ready to stir together. One hour before the party, put the rice in the oven and start the vegetables. Both hold up well. Thirty minutes before the guests assemble, stir together the biscuits and put then in the muffin tins. The crab cakes and the biscuits can be in the oven at the same time— about fifteen minutes before you are ready to serve them.

Beef-lover's Birthday Party

Prepare the Shrimp Paste and Coconut Cake one day in advance. The Brown Rice and Onion au Gratin can bake while someone grills the meat. The salad can be tossed while the Sour Cream Biscuits are baking.

Rum Punch

If you have young guests, they can enjoy the punch without the rum! They always love any beverage with a cherry in it.

Per drink:

2 ounces dark rum

1 ounce cranberry juice

1 ounce pineapple juice

1/8 teaspoon maraschino cherry juice

1/2 to 1 tablespoon fresh lime juice

Lemons to float in drinks

Maraschino cherries, for young guests

Combine ingredients. Increase amounts according to number of guests. Mix drinks and garnish with lemons or cherries.

Sour Cream Biscuits   Makes 1 1/2 dozen

People love these little biscuits because they are the perfect size—you can polish one off in two bites.

2 cups self-rising flour

1 cup (2 sticks) butter, at room
   temperature

1 cup sour cream

Preheat the oven to 400 degrees F. Spray miniature muffin pans with vegetable cooking spray. Mix the flour and butter with a fork. Add sour cream and stir with a fork until well-blended. Spoon batter into miniature muffin pans. Bake for 8 to 10 minutes. Serve hot with butter.

Crab Cakes Serves 8

People love these because they are filled with crabmeat, not fillers.

1 tablespoon butter

1 green onion, finely chopped

1 clove garlic, pressed

2 tablespoons red bell pepper, finely
   chopped

Cayenne pepper to taste

3 tablespoons heavy cream

1 tablespoon Dijon mustard

1 egg

1/2 teaspoon minced parsley

1/2 cup bread crumbs

1 pound white or claw crab meat,
   picked through twice for shells

Topping:

1/2 cup bread crumbs

1/2 cup grated Parmesan cheese

To Sauté or Bake:

2 tablespoons oil

2 tablespoons butter

Lemon Dill Sauce:

1 cup mayonnaise

1/4 cup buttermilk

2 tablespoons chopped fresh dill

1 tablespoon minced parsley

2 teaspoons lemon juice

1 tablespoon grated lemon peel

1 small garlic clove, minced

In a large pan, sauté onion, garlic, and bell pepper in butter until pepper is limp, about 3 minutes. Add cayenne, cream, and mustard. Mix well. Add egg, parsley, and 1/2 cup of bread crumbs. Mix well. Spread crab out onto a baking sheet and pick through carefully for shells. Spreading it out helps you see any shells you might otherwise miss. Gently fold crab into vegetable mixture.

Form into eight patties, about 1/2 inch thick. Combine bread crumbs and Parmesan cheese. Pat topping onto both sides of patties. Refrigerate, covered, in a flat container until firm, at least 2 hours.

Combine oil and butter in heavy-bottomed skillet or an electric skillet. Heat to medium high. Sauté crab cakes in hot oil/butter mixture for about 3 minutes on each side. Or, place patties on cookie sheet. Dribble with oil and butter mixture. Bake at 400 degrees for 10 to 12 minutes.

Serve with lemon dill sauce.

To make the lemon dill sauce: Combine all ingredients in a small container with tight-fitting lid. Chill. Mixture will thicken as it chills. Place a dollop beside crab cakes. Pass extra sauce.

Summer Vegetable Stir Fry Serves 8

This is a fabulous recipe that goes with just about anything. It also happens to be very good for you, full of bright vegetables that are full of anti-oxidants. If you have leftovers, toss them with hot pasta and pass with more Parmesan cheese. Delicious!

2 tablespoons olive oil

2 zucchini, pared lightly and sliced
   into 1-inch sticks

1 or 2 yellow squash, pared lightly
   and sliced into 1/4-inch rounds

1 large onion, cut in slivers

1 large green pepper, cut in strips

1 large red pepper, cut in strips

1 large yellow pepper, cut in strips

1 garlic clove, minced

1 (14-ounce) can whole tomatoes,
   roughly chopped, with juice, or 1 can
   diced tomatoes, with juice

3 tablespoons parsley, washed and
   chopped

1 tablespoon fresh dill, chopped

1 tablespoon fresh basil, chopped

1/4 cup Parmesan cheese, grated

In large stir-fry pan, sauté zucchini, squash, onion, peppers, and garlic in olive oil until vegetables begin to soften, about 5 minutes. Add tomatoes and juice. Sprinkle on herbs. With pan uncovered, allow mixture to simmer over low heat about 10 minutes more. Turn off heat. Sprinkle on Parmesan cheese.

   Serve immediately.

Shrimp Paste Serves 8 to 10

This is an old Savannah recipe that features finely chopped shrimp barely held together with a little butter, cream cheese, and mayonnaise. Yum.

2 pounds shrimp, cooked and cleaned	2 tablespoons mayonnaise
1/2 cup butter, softened	1 teaspoon Worcestershire sauce
1 teaspoon lemon juice	Salt and pepper to taste
1 (8-ounce) package cream cheese, softened	

Roughly chop shrimp in food processor, or by hand. Add remaining ingredients and blend by hand. Mold in 3-cup mold, greased lightly with mayonnaise. Serve with bland crackers.

••

Red Rice Serves 6 to 8

This dish is a Savannah trademark, often served at picnics with fried chicken and at Low Country boils with boiled shrimp. Some people add sliced smoked sausage and serve it as a main course.

4 slices bacon, fried crisp, crumbled and reserved	1 (14-ounce) can tomatoes, undrained
1 onion, chopped	3/4 cup water
1/2 bell pepper, chopped	1 teaspoon salt
1 stalk celery, chopped	1/4 teaspoon cayenne pepper
1 cup raw rice	1/2 teaspoon Tabasco
	1 tablespoon Worcestershire sauce

In a large skillet, sauté onion, bell pepper, and celery in 1 tablespoon bacon grease. Add rice, tomatoes, water, salt, cayenne, Tabasco, and Worcestershire sauce. Stir well. Transfer to 1 1/2-quart baking dish. Cover with foil. Bake at 350 degrees F for 30 minutes. Stir in reserved bacon.

Serve hot, or at room temperature.

Dry-rubbed Tenderloin   Serves 6

I love the taste of beef, mushrooms, and onions—and these next dishes feature that trio. You'll need something green, so I suggest a small salad with flavors bold enough to stand up to the beef and onions.

1 (5-pound) beef tenderloin
1/4 teaspoon garlic salt
1/4 teaspoon celery salt

1/4 teaspoon onion salt
1/4 teaspoon pepper

Combine dry ingredients. Rub mixture into meat. Allow to sit in covered glass dish in refrigerator overnight. Grill meat over hot coals about 30 minutes, or until thickest portion registers 140 degrees F on a meat thermometer. Or, roast in oven 15 minutes at 550 degrees F, reduce temperature to 350 degrees F and continue roasting for 20 minutes. (Meat will be very pink in the middle and less pink on the ends. Roast additional 10 minutes if meat is too rare.) Allow to sit for at least 15 minutes before slicing. Serve each guest several thin slices.

•••

Brown Rice   Serves 4 to 6

You can't miss with this one. It's quick and easy, tastes good, and reheats well.

1 cup raw rice
2 tablespoons butter or margarine
1 (10 1/4-ounce) can beef consomme
1 (10 1/4-ounce) can French onion soup

4 ounces mushrooms, sliced and
   sautéed in additional butter
Pepper to taste

Preheat oven to 350 degrees F. In a medium sauce pan, sauté rice in butter. Stir in other ingredients. Pepper to taste, but do not salt, as soups are already salty. Transfer to greased 2-quart baking dish. Bake, covered, at 350 degrees F for 1 hour.

Coconut Pound Cake   Serves 12 to 16

Buttery rich and full of coconut, this cake is a treat for family or friends. It came from Savannah's Dale Morgan, one of the best cooks I know. I've served it with ice cream, with whipped cream, and all by itself!

2 cups (4 sticks) butter or margarine
2 cups sugar
2 cups all-purpose flour
6 eggs
1 (7-ounce) can of flaked coconut
1 teaspoon vanilla extract

Glaze:
1 cup sugar
1/2 cup water
1 teaspoon coconut flavoring

Whipped Cream
Sliced sweetened strawberries, for
   garnish

Grease and flour a tube or Bundt pan. Preheat oven to 350 degrees F.

Cream butter and sugar for 7 minutes in a large mixing bowl. Add 1 cup flour and mix well. Add eggs one at a time and mix. Add coconut with remaining 1 cup of flour. Mix well. Add vanilla. Spoon batter into tube pan; smooth the top. Tap the pan on the counter to get out any air pockets. Bake in the bottom third of the oven for 1 hour and 15 minutes.

Remove the cake from the oven. Allow it to sit in the pan for about 10 minutes.

To make the glaze: Simmer all ingredients for 10 minutes in a small saucepan.

Spoon a little glaze evenly over the top of the cake. Loosen the sides of the cake with a table knife and then turn out onto a cooling rack with waxed paper underneath to catch the drippings of the glaze. Pierce the top of cake all over with a fork. Spoon glaze over cake. Cool completely on wire rack. Serve at room temperature with sliced sweetened strawberries and whipped cream.

Cake freezes well. Wrap in plastic wrap and place the entire cake in a large freezer bag.

Onions Au Gratin   Serves 6

Vidalia onions are grown near Savannah and they are eagerly anticipated by onion lovers each May. The Georgia soil they are grown in make the onions sweet, and they are particularly delicious baked.

2 large Vidalia onions	3 tablespoons butter or margarine,
3/4 cup chicken broth, homemade	divided
or canned	1/2 cup soft bread crumbs
1/4 teaspoon thyme	1/4 cup grated sharp Cheddar cheese
Salt and pepper to taste	

Preheat oven to 400 degrees F. Slice onions and arrange in baking dish, overlapping slices. Pour broth over onions. Sprinkle with thyme, salt if needed, pepper and dot with 1 tablespoon butter.

Bake, covered, at 400 degrees F for 25 minutes. Toss bread crumbs in remaining 2 tablespoons butter, melted. Combine cheese with bread crumbs. Sprinkle mixture over onions.

Bake at 400 degrees F for an additional 10 minutes.

Apple-Pecan-Bleu Cheese Salad   Serves 6

This has beautiful color and is a nice counterpoint to the robust flavors of the rest of the beef menu.

1 Romaine heart, chopped	**Dressing:**
1 green apple, skin left on, thinly sliced	1/2 cup canola oil
1/2 cup pecan pieces, toasted until	2 tablespoons red wine vinegar
just brown	1/4 cup sugar
4 ounces bleu cheese, crumbled	

Combine salad ingredients. Combine dressing ingredients. Toss just before serving.

Beach Picnic

Something happens to you the minute you hit the beach—you become ravenous! I have, on occasion, eaten lunch at 10 a.m. on beach outings. I just can't wait to get into the food! Now that I know about UV rays, we don't do much all-day sunning anymore; instead, we're more apt to spread the picnic blanket about 3 p.m. and stay until the beach becomes deserted and the sun is a little less brazen. This menu works well as either a picnic lunch or supper.

In selecting the menu items, I went for some bold flavors—beef tenderloin rolled around tangy horseradish sauce, a zesty potato salad, tomato muffins with sautéed onions and herbs, and several appetizers and desserts to keep your guests content during a long afternoon.

You'll need to think things through so that you don't end up on the beach without the utensils you will need to enjoy the meal—make sure to keep one large blanket free from sand so you'll have a nice place to plop with your plate. Be sure to add serving pieces and antibacterial wipes to the list, along with plates, forks, napkins, and plenty of delicious lemonade.

Tips

Nothing tastes good with sand as an ingredient, so take care to keep the food in plastic bags and containers with snap-on lids.

Don't let your guests put their sandy hands in the bags—plate the food yourself and serve it.

This menu is full of flavor, texture and color—the Beef Roll, Broccoli Salad, and the Pimiento Cheese make for a colorful picnic plate.

Pineapple Nut Tea Sandwiches Makes 3 dozen

Pineapple sandwiches are on most tea party menus in the South, and they travel well for warm-weather picnics, too. Anne Coakley shared this treasured recipe.

2 cups crushed pineapple, drained
1 cup sugar
1 cup chopped pecans

8 ounces of cream cheese, softened
1 tablespoon milk or mayonnaise

In saucepan, combine pineapple and sugar. Bring to a boil. Cook until thick, stirring constantly. Stir in nuts. Combine cream cheese with milk or mayonnaise to make a good spreading consistency. Combine pineapple and cream cheese. Spread on thin bread and add a top. Trim off crusts and cut into diagonals.

Lemonade Makes 1 gallon

Fresh lemon juice makes the best lemonade.

2 cups lemon juice, plus extra
   lemon slices
2 cups sugar
Water, to fill a gallon container

Dissolve sugar in 2 cups of hot water. Then mix the sugar syrup, and lemon juice with enough water to fill a gallon container. Keep chilled. Have extra lemon slices to float in lemonade.

Tenderloin Rolls   Serves 6 to 8

2 pounds tenderloin, rubbed with salt, pepper and garlic powder and grilled until 140 degrees in the thickest part of the meat

4 ounces cream cheese, softened

4 tablespoons sour cream

1 tablespoon finely minced green pepper

1 tablespoon minced green onion

1 teaspoon salt

1 tablespoon prepared horseradish

Allow tenderloin to cool completely. Slice very thinly.

Combine cream cheese, sour cream, green pepper, green onion, salt, and horseradish. Spread a thin layer onto each slice of meat and roll up tightly. Secure with a toothpick.

Place beef rolls into an airtight container. Keep chilled until ready to eat.

Gary's Pimiento Cheese   Makes 8 to 10 sandwiches

Gary is my husband and this recipe is his claim to fame. It's fantastic on toast, too.

1 (8-ounce) package shredded sharp Cheddar cheese

1 (8-ounce) package of cream cheese

1/4 cup mayonnaise

1 (2-ounce) jar of pimientos, with a little juice

Allow cheeses to come to room temperature. In a medium bowl, combine cheeses with mayonnaise and stir well. Stir in pimientos and a little juice (about a teaspoon). Spread on fresh bakery bread and package sandwiches in individual sandwich bags. Or, stuff into celery sticks and store in an airtight container.

Broccoli Salad, Sweet and Sour Dressing Serves 8 to 10

Dressing:
1 large whole egg
1/2 cup sugar
1/2 teaspoon dry mustard
1 1/2 teaspoons cornstarch
1/4 cup white vinegar
1/4 cup water
1/4 teaspoon salt
1/2 cup mayonnaise

2 tablespoons butter or margarine,
  softened

Salad:
4 cups broccoli flowerettes
1 cup raisins
1/2 cup chopped purple onion
4 to 6 slices bacon, cooked and crumbled

For dressing: Whisk together the egg, sugar, mustard, and cornstarch. In saucepan, combine vinegar, water, and salt and bring to boil. Whisk in egg mixture and cook for about 1 minute, or until thickened, whisking constantly. Remove pan from heat and whisk in butter. Add mayonnaise; stir. Chill dressing in covered container.

To make salad: Combine salad ingredients. Pour dressing over salad just before serving. Toss well.

Black Bean and Corn Salsa Makes about 4 cups

1 can black beans, rinsed and drained
1 1/2 cups frozen whole kernel corn
  (uncooked)
4 Roma tomatoes, diced
1/2 green pepper, diced
1/2 red onion, minced
2 garlic cloves
Juice of 2 limes

1 tablespoon red wine or
  balsamic vinegar
1 tablespoon extra-virgin olive oil
1 teaspoon cumin
1 teaspoon Creole seasoning
1 teaspoons Texas Pete Pepper Sauce
4 tablespoons fresh cilantro, finely
  minced

Combine ingredients and store in container with snap-on lid. Keep chilled. Serve with corn chips.

Horseradish Potato Salad   Serves 8 to 10

This should not be confused with the mild-mannered potato salad on page 56. This salad is robust and spicy—probably not for the kids.

1 cup mayonnaise

1/2 cup sour cream

1 1/2 teaspoons horseradish, or more, to taste

1/2 teaspoon celery seed

1/2 teaspoon salt

1/4 teaspoon pepper

8 medium potatoes or 8 medium new potatoes, sliced into 1/2 inch slices and boiled in salted water until tender, but not mushy

1/2 cup parsley, washed, dried, and chopped

1/2 cup chopped green onion

Additional parsley and onion for garnish

Combine mayonnaise, sour cream, horseradish, celery seed, salt, and pepper. Set aside.

Place half of the potatoes in a medium bowl; sprinkle with 1 1/2 tablespoons each parsley and onion. Cover with half of the mayonnaise mixture. Do not stir. Repeat layers, ending with a layer of mayonnaise mixture that completely covers top so no air reaches potatoes.

Garnish with a little remaining parsley and onion. Store in an airtight container with a plastic lid. When ready to serve, stir entire mixture together.

Note: Can be made up to 12 hours ahead of serving time.

Tomato Herb Muffins Makes 12 muffins

The South has many culinary stars, but great tomatoes are somewhere near the top of the list. During tomato season, many Southerners eat tomato sandwiches for dinner!

2 cups all-purpose flour
1 tablespoon baking powder
1/2 teaspoon salt
1/4 teaspoon freshly ground pepper
1 cup milk
1 egg
1/4 cup olive oil
1/2 cup freshly grated Parmesan cheese
1/4 cup finely chopped fresh tomatoes, drained
1/4 cup finely chopped Vidalia onions,

sautéed in butter until limp
2 teaspoons finely chopped (basil, tarragon, or rosemary) herbs

Tomato-Herb Butter:
1 tablespoon tomato paste
4 tablespoons (1/2 stick) butter
1 teaspoon finely chopped (basil, tarragon, or rosemary) herbs

Preheat oven to 375 degrees F. In a large bowl, stir together flour, baking powder, salt and pepper. In medium bowl, whisk together milk, egg, and olive oil. Add cheese, tomatoes, onions, and herbs to dry mixture. Combine wet and dry ingredients; stir just till blended.

Spoon into prepared muffin tins, filled three-quarters full. Bake until a toothpick inserted in center of muffins comes out clean, about 20 minutes. Cool in tins for 3 minutes. Remove.

To make the **tomato-herb butter**: Combine butter and about a tablespoon of tomato paste, along with finely chopped fresh herbs of your choice—basil, tarragon or rosemary.

Lemon Bars Makes 32

This is a favorite recipe for tart lemon bars, and is perfect with the tangy beef and potato salad.

1 cup butter or margarine, melted	2 cups sugar
2 cups all-purpose flour, plus	1 teaspoon baking powder
4 tablespoons flour	6 tablespoons fresh lemon juice
1 cup confectioners' sugar	Additional confectioners' sugar for
4 eggs	dusting bars

Preheat oven to 350 degrees F. Combine butter, 2 cups flour, and 1 cup confectioners' sugar with wooden spoon. Pat with flour hands into buttered 13 x 9-inch baking pan. Bake for 20 minutes.

While crust is cooling, beat together eggs, sugar, baking powder, remaining flour and lemon juice. Pour over baked crust and bake for an additional 30 to 35 minutes, until filling appears set.

Cool, then sprinkle lightly with confectioners' sugar. Cut in bars. Store in airtight container with tight-fitting lid.

Fudge Brownie Muffins Makes 10

1/2 cup butter or margarine	1 teaspoon vanilla extract
3 tablespoons unsweetened cocoa	3/4 cup all-purpose flour
powder	1/4 cup finely chopped pecans,
2 large eggs, lightly beaten	toasted
1 cup sugar	Semisweet chocolate morsels

Preheat oven to 350 degrees F. Melt butter. Add cocoa. Combine eggs, sugar, and vanilla extract. Beat well. Combine butter mixture, flour, and chopped pecans, stirring until just blended.

Spoon into large muffin cups that have been sprayed with vegetable spray, filling three-quarters full. Sprinkle tops of each muffin with a few chocolate morsels. Bake for 20 minutes. Remove from pans immediately and cool on wire rack. Store in airtight container with snap-on lid. Muffins freeze well.

St. Patrick's
Day Buffet

In Savannah, everyone turns Irish at least once a year, on St. Patrick's Day. These dishes, however, are delicious any time you decide to serve them.

The festivities on St. Patrick's Day in Savannah, which boasts one of the largest parades in the nation, start early. Seasoned parade-goers set up their viewing stations in the downtown squares at daybreak, often breaking into the picnic baskets by mid-morning. That's a great time to serve grilled reubens—corned beef, sauerkraut, and Swiss grilled on rye bread. (Try the potato salad from the beach picnic menu). Meanwhile, back at home, have the corned beef and potatoes cooking in a crock pot or slow roasting in the oven so that the aroma hits you when you open the door after you've come in from a long morning of float-, band- and soldier-watching.

Corned beef was popular with Irish immigrants who settled in New York and Boston at the turn of the century because it was 5 cents a portion, making it an affordable feast. Before refrigeration, boneless cuts of beef were embedded or sprinkled with "corns of salt" to preserve them. Later, brining or pickling took the place of the salting, but the term "corned beef" stuck.

Irish Soda Muffins Makes 24

The white cheddar and rosemary give these muffins an intense flavor that complements both the Irish Stew or the Corned Beef and Cabbage.

3 cups all-purpose flour

1 cup whole wheat flour

2 teaspoons baking powder

1 1/2 teaspoons salt

1 teaspoon baking soda

1/4 cup (1/2 stick) well-chilled butter, cut into pieces

6 ounces coarsely grated white Cheddar cheese

1/4 cup fresh rosemary, snipped finely with kitchen shears

2 cups buttermilk

1 egg, beaten to blend

Preheat oven to 350 degrees F. Generously grease 2 (12-cup) muffin tins. Sift together flours, baking powder, salt, and baking soda in large bowl. Cut in butter until mixture resembles coarse meal. Stir in cheese and rosemary. Mix buttermilk and egg and add to dry ingredients, stirring just until blended (batter will be thick). Spoon batter into prepared muffin tins. Bake until golden, about 20 minutes. Serve warm.

To freeze, cool thoroughly. Wrap tightly in aluminum foil and place in freezer baggies. To serve, bring to room temperature. Warm in oven for about 15 minutes at 300 degrees F just before serving.

Reubens Makes 8 large sandwiches

This is my favorite Sunday lunch sandwich, served with tomato soup.

1/2 cup mayonnaise

2 tablespoons chili sauce

1 tablespoon horseradish

2 teaspoons Dijon mustard

Seedless rye bread

2 pounds thinly sliced deli corned beef

1 cup sauerkraut, drained

8 thick slices Swiss cheese

1/4 cup softened butter

Combine mayonnaise, chili sauce, horseradish, and mustard. Set aside. Spread sauce lightly on both sides of bread. Layer corned beef, Swiss cheese, and tablespoon of sauerkraut. Lightly brush both sides of bread with softened butter. Grill as if you are making grilled cheese sandwiches. Cut sandwiches in half, wrap in foil, and place in a large plastic bag.

Spinach and Apple Salad Serves 8

This is great for any spring meal. It's also delicious made with Bibb lettuce.

10 ounces fresh spinach, washed and
   dried, stems removed

1 cup red onion rings, thinly sliced

1 cup pecans, coarsely chopped

1 Granny Smith apple, cored and
   thinly sliced

Dressing:

3 tablespoons lemon juice

1/2 cup vegetable oil

2 tablespoons sugar

1 small clove garlic, crushed

1 teaspoon salt

Whisk together dressing ingredients in a small bowl. Place spinach leaves on plates and top with red onion rings, pecans, and apple slices. Pour dressing over each serving.

Corned Beef and New Potatoes Serves 6

The delicious corned beef flavors the potatoes.

1 (4 to 5 pound) corned beef	1/2 cup water
12 medium new potatoes	1/2 teaspoon pepper
1 cup liquid from corned beef	

Spray a large crock pot with vegetable cooking spray. Quarter the potatoes in the bottom of the crock pot. Place the corned beef on top, and pour in the liquids. Sprinkle with pepper. Cook on low 7-8 hours.

Or, spray a large Dutch oven with vegetable cooking spray. Place corned beef in the oven and place the potatoes around the meat. Add corned beef liquid and water. Season with pepper. Cover and cook at 350 degrees for 3 ½ hours, until meat is very tender.

Allow meat to sit for at least 15 minutes before slicing thinly across the grain.

Note: You can cook the cabbage with the meat and potatoes, but I find that the cabbage over-cooks. I prefer it as a separate dish.

Steamed Cabbage Serves 6 to 8

I adore cabbage steamed, with just a touch of butter.

3/4 head of cabbage, thinly sliced	2 tablespoons butter
1 teaspoon salt	Ground pepper to taste
1/2 cup water	

Bring water, salt, and cabbage to a boil in a large saucepan; place lid on pan and steam cabbage about 10 minutes, or until tender.

Remove from heat. Stir in butter until melted. Season with pepper. Serve immediately.

Irish Stew   Serves 8

3 pounds leg-of-lamb meat,
   cut into 1 1/2 -inch squares

Salt and pepper

Flour for dredging

1/4 cup Canola oil

1/4 cup olive oil

4 celery stalks, chopped, including
   tops and leaves

2 large Spanish onions, chopped

2 cups chopped leeks

1/2 small head of cabbage, shredded

1 teaspoon ground thyme

2 (14 1/2-ounce) cans of beef broth

1 (14 1/2-ounce) can diced tomatoes,
drained, juice reserved

4 large baking potatoes, peeled and
   quartered

Preheat oven to 300 degrees F. Wash the lamb chunks and pat dry. Dredge in flour. In a large Dutch oven, sauté the lamb chunks in the oils until browned. Add the celery, onions, leeks, cabbage, thyme, broth, and tomatoes. Cover and bake for 1 hour.

Peel and quarter the potatoes and add them to the stew. Cook for 1 hour more, until meat is tender and potatoes are soft.

Crème de Menthe Parfaits   Makes 8

You'll need room in the freezer to store these, but your guests will be so glad you went to the trouble of cleaning out the freezer!

1 package chocolate wafer cookies, crushed
1/2 gallon vanilla ice cream
1/2 cup crème de menthe
Additional cup crème de menthe (for garnish)
1 cup heavy cream, whipped
Mint leaves or chocolate mint candy

Thaw ice cream until soft, about 15 minutes. Mix 1/2 cup crème de menthe with ice cream in a large mixing bowl.

In small parfait glasses, alternate layers of crushed wafers and ice cream. Cover each parfait with plastic wrap. Place the glasses in a cake pan so they will have support. Freeze. When ready to serve, top with dollop of whipped cream and dribble crème de menthe over whipped cream. Garnish with mint leaves or chocolate mint candy.

Irish Coffee

For each cup:

Lemon slice

Sugar, enough to coat rim of glass

$1/2$ to 1 ounce Irish whiskey

$1/2$ to $3/4$ cup hot, strong black coffee

1-2 teaspoons sugar

Rub lemon slice around rim of glass mug. Dip mug in sugar to coat rim of glass. Pour in coffee. Add sugar and stir. Add whiskey. Slide whipped cream off of spoon so that it floats on top of coffee. Do not stir—sip the coffee "through" the cream, which flavors it. Garnish with mint if desired.

Oyster Roast

I had never been to an oyster roast until I moved to Savannah as a twenty-something. I had attended some of Savannah's fanciest soirees, and so was surprised to discover this most casual style of outdoor dining. Oyster roasts are held most often in the coldest months, when oysters are at their best. No matter who you are, the oyster roast dress code is jeans and a sweater that you don't mind getting muddy—and, if you are a real pro, you'll have an oyster glove and oyster knife in your back pocket.

Singles or clusters are roasted over a sturdy piece of steel placed over a roaring fire. The oysters are covered with a burlap sack, which is hosed down; the oysters steam underneath. The oysters are ready when they pop open; the oyster cookers have the responsibility of making that call, as well as the chore of shoveling the oysters from the fire to the table, which is usually wooden, at least waist high, and unadorned. Oysters also can be steamed in large pots, which is easier and offers more control than roasting them over an open fire.

Crackers, melted butter, and cocktail sauce are the oyster's accompaniments.

There are always a few folks who don't eat roasted oysters, and for them, we have a Plains Cheese Ring to serve as an appetizer. You will be pleasantly surprised at the way the unlikely ingredients taste!

When everyone has had their fill of the outdoors, invite your guests inside to the kitchen, where you'll have pots of soup on the stove and a taco salad on the counter, as well as several yummy desserts on the sideboard. This is a serve-yourself meal, and, along with the Low Country Boil, is probably Savannah's most casual way to throw a big party.

Plains Cheese Ring   Serves 12 to 16

Former First Lady Rosalynn Carter is given credit for making this addictive spread popular. It was one of Jimmy's favorites and was always on the Carter family's holiday table. This is my version.

---

1 pound sharp Cheddar cheese,
  grated, then allowed to soften
1 cup chopped pecans
1 cup mayonnaise
1 small onion, grated

1/2 teaspoon black pepper to taste
Dash cayenne
Strawberry preserves, your favorite
  brand

Combine the cheese, pecans, mayonnaise, onion, black pepper, and cayenne. Pulse in a food processor until blended. Place in a 2-quart ring mold, greased with a little mayonnaise. Chill.

When ready to serve, unmold. Fill center with preserves.

Serve with a favorite cracker. The spread is also delicious stuffed into celery sticks.

Clockwise from bottom: Chili, Clam Chowder, Wild Rice Soup, and Chunky Tomato Soup

Chili Serves 4 to 6

I had always made chili with kidney beans until a few years ago when I began to use black beans instead. My family now prefers the black beans. This is also great made with ground venison. This recipe serves four. Double the recipe if you're having a crowd.

3 tablespoons butter or margarine

1 large onion, chopped

1 green pepper, chopped

2 cloves garlic, pressed or minced

1 pound ground beef

1 (14 1/2-ounce) can diced tomatoes

1 (14 1/2-ounce) can filled with water

1 (8-ounce) can tomato sauce

1 teaspoon celery seed

1/2 teaspoon cayenne pepper

2 tablespoons chili powder

1 teaspoon dried basil

1 1/2 teaspoons salt

1 (14 1/2-ounce) can kidney beans or
  black beans

Garnish:

Corn chips

Sour cream

Green onions, chopped

Cheddar cheese, grated

In large Dutch oven, sauté onion, green pepper, and garlic in butter for about a minute. Add ground beef and brown. Drain off fat.

Add all other ingredients except beans and bring to a boil. Reduce heat and allow to simmer about 2 hours, uncovered, until sauce is very thick. Add beans about 10 minutes before serving.

Have bowls of corn chips, sour cream, chopped green onions, and grated Cheddar cheese for garnish.

Sweet Corn Chowder   Serves 8 to 10

The original corn chowder recipe came from Elizabeth on 37th Restaurant. I discovered that I could add a can of celery soup at the end and stretch it further with no real difference in the made-from-scratch taste.

1/2 cup celery, minced

1/2 cup onion, minced

1/2 cup leek, white part only, minced

1/2 cup green onion, minced

2 medium baking potatoes, peeled and
   minced

2 tablespoons butter

4 cups chicken broth

4 ears of sweet corn, kernels removed
from the cob with a sharp paring knife

1/4 cup red bell pepper, minced

1/2 cup heavy cream

1 (10 1/2-ounce) can cream of celery soup

Dash of cayenne

Salt to taste

Garnish:

4 slices bacon, cooked crisp, crumbled

4 tablespoons minced fresh chives

Place celery, onion, leek, green onion, potatoes, and butter in a large covered saucepan over very low heat for about 5 minutes, stirring constantly, until vegetables cook slightly. Add chicken stock and simmer for 15 minutes, until vegetables are soft. Add corn to chowder. Add bell pepper. Simmer 10 minutes more. Add heavy cream and cream of celery soup. Taste, and then add cayenne and salt, if needed.

Just before serving, top each bowl of chowder with crumbled bacon and minced chives.

Chunky Tomato Soup 8 to 10

This recipe ran in Savannah Magazine, and readers raved. If you'd like, you can puree the soup in batches in a blender or food processor and add a sprinkling of Parmesan. This turns the soup into a smooth, sophisticated first course suitable for a fancy dinner party.

1/2 cup (1 stick) butter

1/4 cup all-purpose flour

1 large onion, diced

2 cloves garlic, diced

4 cups chicken broth

2 (8-ounce) cans of tomato sauce

1 (29-ounce) can diced tomatoes,
 with their juice

1 teaspoon hot sauce, such as
 Texas Pete

1/4 cup honey

2 teaspoons dried dill weed

1/2 teaspoon black pepper

2 teaspoons chili powder

2 teaspoons dried basil

Garnish:

1/2 cup croutons

1 cup grated Cheddar

1 cup sour cream

6 slices crisply fried bacon, crumbled

In a heavy saucepan, melt 4 tablespoons butter. Whisk in flour and stir until smooth. Cook over very low heat for about three minutes, until thick. In a separate small skillet, melt the rest of the butter and sauté the onion and garlic over low heat until very soft, about five minutes. Add onions to the flour mixture. Whisk well. Over low heat, slowly whisk in the chicken broth, one cup at a time, allowing the soup to thicken after each cup. Add the rest of the ingredients, and stir well.

Turn off the heat and allow soup to come to room temperature. Refrigerate overnight. When ready to serve, allow the soup to sit on the counter for 15 minutes to take off the chill, then heat gently over low heat for 30 minutes so flavors can blend.

Serve with croutons, grated Cheddar, sour cream, and crispy fried bacon bits.

Sherried Wild Rice Soup   Makes 6 cups

Wild rice as a real luxury. This soup blends the unique rice flavor into a delicious, sherry-laced broth.

2 tablespoons butter

1 tablespoon minced onion

1/4 cup all-purpose flour

4 cups chicken stock

1 1/2 cups cooked wild rice

1/2 teaspoon salt

1 cup half-and-half

1/4 cup dry sherry

Garnish:

Parsley, washed, dried and minced

Melt butter in a 2-quart pot. Add onion and cook until soft, about 5 minutes. Blend in flour; slowly add broth, whisking constantly until thickened. Stir in rice and salt. Simmer for 5 minutes. Blend in half-and-half and sherry. Heat but do not boil. Garnish with parsley.

Sweet and Savory Cornbread   Serves 8

Great with soups! Bake this cornbread in a cake pan and serve slices, or in a square pan to cut into squares.

2 eggs

1 (8-ounce) can creamed corn

1/2 cup melted butter

1/2 cup sugar

1 cup all-purpose flour

1 cup stone-ground corn meal

3 tablespoons baking powder

1 (4-ounce) can green chilis, drained

1 cup sharp Cheddar cheese

Heat oven to 375 degrees F. In a large bowl, whisk the eggs. Add the corn and whisk. Add the batter and sugar, and whisk again. In a separate bowl, combine the flour, cornmeal, and baking powder. Stir with a spoon into the egg mixture. Add the chilis and cheese and stir. Soon the mixture into a 9-inch round cake pan, or a 9-inch square pan, sprayed with vegetable cooking pray. Smooth top. Bake 30 to 35 minutes, until set.

New England Clam Chowder Makes 6 cups

Our family had fabulous clam chowder in Seattle before catching a ship to Alaska in 2007. I was determined to create a recipe that was close to what we had enjoyed, and here it is.

4 pieces of lean bacon, finely diced	2 tablespoons butter
1 small onion, finely chopped	2 tablespoons all-purpose flour
3 ribs of celery, finely chopped	1 cup half-and-half
1 (8-ounce) bottle of clam juice	2 (8-ounce) can of clams, with juice
1 cup of chicken broth	1/2 teaspoon salt
2 small white potatoes, peeled and diced	1/4 teaspoon pepper
	Oyster crackers

In a heavy bottomed 2-quart saucepan, cook the bacon over medium heat until it is very crisp. Remove the bacon and reserve. Drain all but 1 tablespoon of the bacon grease. Sauté the onion and the celery in the bacon grease over low heat until it is very tender, about 8 minutes. Add the clam juice, the chicken broth, and the white potatoes, and cook over medium-low heat until potato is tender, about 15 minutes.

In a small saucepan, melt the butter. Whisk in the flour. Add the half-and-half and cook until the white sauce is thick. Stir it into the vegetables and stock. Add the clams. Stir. Turn off heat. Add the salt and pepper. Stir in the reserved bacon.

Serve with oyster crackers.

Taco Salad   Serves 8 to 10

Whenever I need a guaranteed hit, I turn to this old favorite. It hasn't lost its appeal in the 40 years since I first began serving it. My sister-in-law, Linda Giddens, discovered the recipe long before Mexican dishes were the rage, and it was my standard when I was 18 and began giving graduation luncheons!

1 pound ground beef, browned, crumbled, and drained

2 ripe tomatoes, diced

8 ounces sharp Cheddar cheese, diced or grated

1 large sweet onion, chopped

1 medium head iceberg lettuce, washed, drained, and chopped

1 (16-ounce) bottle Catalina dressing

1 (7-ounce) bag original taco-flavored chips, crushed

1 (8-ounce) jar mild or medium taco sauce

Fresh cilantro, chopped, for garnish

Cook the ground beef, drain, and store in a plastic bag in the refrigerator until ready to use. Chop the tomatoes, cheese, onion, and lettuce and store each ingredient separately in plastic bags. When ready to prepare the salad, heat the ground beef in the plastic bag, unsealed, for 30 seconds in the microwave on high, to take off the chill.

In a large salad bowl, combine the tomatoes, cheese, onion, lettuce, and ground beef. A few minutes before serving, pour entire bottle of dressing over salad ingredients and mix well. Just before serving add taco-flavored chips, tossing to combine with other ingredients. Stir in the taco sauce. Garnish salad with cilantro.

Serve immediately. Have extra cilantro for garnish.

Savannah Squares Makes 48 pieces

During the Gulf War, Pat Hackney, a home economist in Savannah, had the idea of preparing and delivering Savannah Squares to the 20,000 troops from the 24th Infantry who were deployed in the Gulf from Savannah. She coordinated 1,000 volunteers who cooked and packaged the mailing of five tons of Savannah Squares in one day. Pat and nine other United Way volunteers personally delivered the Savannah Squares to the U.S. troops stationed in Saudi Arabia.

1 cup (2 sticks) butter, at room temperature
1 cup firmly packed light brown sugar
3/4 cup granulated sugar
1 teaspoon vanilla extract

2 large eggs
2 1/2 cups self-rising flour
6 ounces semi-sweet chocolate morsels
1/2 cup chopped pecans

Preheat the oven to 375 degrees F.

Cream the butter, sugars, and vanilla until smooth. Beat in eggs. Gradually add flour and stir until it is incorporated into the butter mixture. Stir in morsels and nuts.

Spread the dough into a 15 1/2 x 10 1/2 x 1-inch baking pan. Bake for 20 to 25 minutes. Cool for 15 minutes. Cut into 48 pieces. The squares will be very thin but very delicious!

··

Almond Crunch Makes 2 cups of candy

My sister-in-law, Debra Nesbit, shared this recipe. It's addictive!

1 cup sliced almonds
6 tablespoons butter

1/2 cup sugar
1 tablespoon light corn syrup

Line bottom and sides of an 8 x 8-inch pan with aluminum foil. Set aside. Combine all ingredients in a 10-inch non-stick skillet. Bring to boil over medium heat, stirring constantly. Boil until mixture turns golden brown, about 8 to 10 minutes. Quickly spread in prepared pan. When completely cool, break into bite-sized pieces. Do not attempt to eat while hot—hot sugar will burn!

Five Flavor Poundcake   Serves 12 to 16

Pound cakes are great at large gatherings because they serve 12 to 16, depending on how thin you cut the slices. The glaze and the five flavors are what set this apart from other poundcake recipes. June Reese, my minister's wife, always brought this to church events at Isle of Hope Methodist.

1 cup (2 sticks) butter	**Glaze:**
1/2 cup Crisco shortening	1 cup sugar
3 cups sugar	1/2 cup water
5 eggs, well beaten	1 teaspoon each coconut, rum, butter,
3 cups all-purpose flour	lemon, and vanilla extracts
1/2 teaspoon baking powder	
1 cup milk	
1 teaspoon each, coconut, rum, butter,	
lemon, and vanilla extracts	

Preheat oven to 325 degrees F. Grease and flour a 10-inch tube pan.

Cream butter, shortening, and sugar with an electric mixer, until light and fluffy. Add well-beaten eggs and blend. Combine flour and baking powder and add to creamed mixture, adding alternately with milk. Begin and end with flour. Add extracts. Spoon batter into pan. Smooth the top. Tap the pan on the countertop several times to get out any air pockets.

Bake cake for 1 1/2 hours, or until tester comes out clean.

To prepare glaze, mix all ingredients in a small saucepan and bring to a boil. Boil 1 minute, until sugar dissolves. Turn off heat.

Remove cake from oven when done. Allow to cool slightly. Spoon glaze over cake in pan while cake is still warm. When completely cool, remove cake from tube pan. Store in a cake container with a tight-fitting lid.

Roasted Oysters Serves 8 to 10

Oysters can be purchased as singles or clusters. The clusters have lots of little oysters for you to discover, and are a little saltier. However, I prefer the singles.

1 bushel oysters	Cocktail sauce
Butter	Saltine crackers

In Savannah, oysters are roasted over a hot, wood fire with a sturdy piece of steel laid over the top. Oysters are spread out in a single layer and a piece of burlap is laid over them. The burlap is hosed down and steam is created as the oysters cook. The oysters pop open, but should never be allowed to burn. This can take 10 to 15 minutes, depending on the fire.

The cooked oysters are removed with a clean shovel and placed on a wooden table.

Each diner will need a cotton glove for the left hand to help them grip the hot oysters, an oyster knife, and butter and cocktail sauce for dipping. Many people like to place the oyster on a Saltine cracker and top with cocktail sauce.

Oysters also can be steamed outside over a gas burner in a large pot, and even on your stovetop at home. Steaming this way takes 8 to 10 minutes. You can also roast a small number of oysters in a roasting pan, covered with a wet kitchen towel, on the grill over hot coals.

Shuck any leftover oysters and refrigerate. They make wonderful oyster stew.

Oyster Stew Serves 4

1 tablespoon butter	1 dozen roasted oysters
1 celery stalk, finely minced	1/2 teaspoon cayenne pepper
1/4 small onion, finely minced	1/2 teaspoon Worcestershire sauce
2 cups (1 pint) half-and-half	1 teaspoon lemon juice

Melt butter in a medium saucepan. Sauté celery and onion over low heat for 5 minutes. Add half-and-half, oysters, cayenne, Worcestershire, and lemon juice. Taste. Salt and pepper if needed. Serve hot.

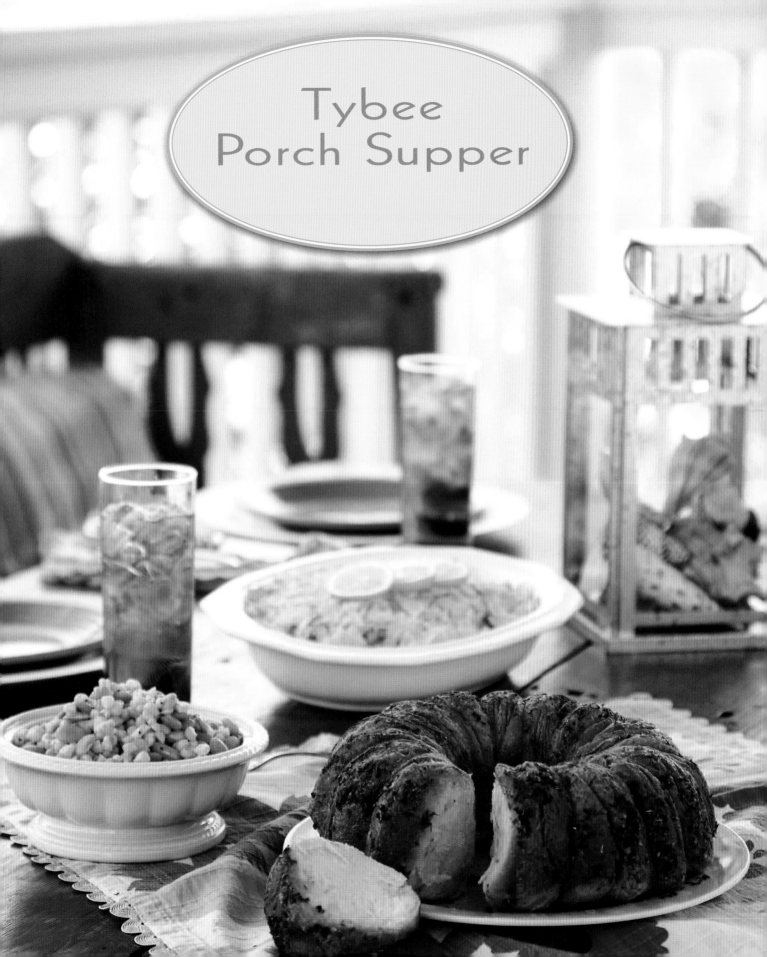

Tybee
Porch Supper

Tybee Island is Savannah's beach, and it raises one's standing in society immensely to say either "I live at Tybee" or "We have a small place at Tybee," meaning that it's a second home. Tybee has managed to hang on to its roots as a beach town. There are no high rises here, but there are some lovely old homes with wrap-around porches to catch the beach breeze and the sound of the Atlantic crashing on the sandy shore, and a number of charming cottages that have been restored and painted pastels and tropical colors.

There are terrific restaurants on Tybee that feature fabulous fried seafood, Low Country boil, steamed oysters and crab, crab cakes, and fish prepared in a number of innovative ways. A great way to entertain at Tybee, however, is to invite someone you just saw walking on the beach over for a casual porch supper. This means that you need a simple meal that requires little attention so that you can concentrate on the conversation and company.

So, here's the plan. Early in the day, you make the salsa, the hot chicken salad, the succotash and the key lime cheesecake. You take a nap. You go for a beach walk around 5 p.m., and invite the best conversationalists (single, couple, or trio) you see on the beach to dinner at 7 p.m.. At 6:30, you chill the wine. At 6:45, you arrange the biscuits in the Bundt pan for the fine-herb roll and light the porch candles. At 7 p.m., when the company arrives, you will bring out the wine and the fresh salsa, remove the cheesecake from the fridge to take off the chill, put the hot chicken salad in the oven, and warm the succotash on the stove top or in the microwave. The aromas coming from your kitchen will say, "I'm so glad you came." You will get raves, I promise.

Any leftover Chicken Salad makes a terrific sandwich the next day.

Fresh Salsa with Corn Chips   Serves 6

This dish screams SUMMER, and is terribly healthy, too, if you don't count the chips. This is our favorite hot-weather treat, and is especially good when tomatoes and bell peppers are at their peak, in June and July. I have, however, made perfectly adequate salsa in winter with quality canned tomatoes.

3 large juicy ripe tomatoes, diced,
    or 1 (14 1/2-ounce) can quality tomatoes,
    chopped and partially drained
1 small onion, finely chopped, or ½ of a
    large Vidalia onion
1 small bell pepper, finely chopped
1 jalapeno pepper, seeded, deveined
    and chopped (use 2 peppers if they
    are very small)

1 (4-ounce) can chopped green chilies
1 clove garlic, minced or pressed
2 tablespoons red wine vinegar
1 tablespoon olive oil
Crisp tortilla chips

Combine everything, except the chips, in a covered crock. Chill if there's time. Serve with plain tortilla chips.

Hot Chicken Salad Serves 4 to 6

This is a favorite at our house, and I never fix it that my husband doesn't remark, "You should make this more often." The recipe is a treasured one, given to me by the late Sally Sullivan, a longtime Savannah caterer and a once-in-a-lifetime character. The secret to the recipe is the large proportion of celery, the lemon juice, and, believe it or not, the potato chips!

2 cups cooked chicken, roughly chopped (one large breast yields about ¾ cup of cooked chicken; boil gently in salted water until done, about 20 minutes)

2 cups (about 6 small stalks) celery, chopped

1 cup mayonnaise

1 cup sharp Cheddar cheese, grated

3 teaspoons lemon juice

1/2 cup slivered almonds

Salt, as needed

1/2 teaspoon freshly ground black pepper

1 1/2 cups crushed potato chips

Combine the chicken, celery, mayonnaise, Cheddar, lemon juice, and almonds. Taste and add salt if needed. Add pepper and stir. Place into a 2-quart casserole, sprayed with vegetable cooking spray. Top with chips. Cover with plastic wrap and keep refrigerated until ready to bake.

Preheat oven to 375 degrees F. Bake for 20 minutes, or until hot and bubbly.

Fine Herb Roll Serves 8 to 10

Two cans of biscuits are transformed into a beautiful bread ring that can be pulled apart. Any leftovers can be toasted for a savory breakfast treat. Use fresh or dried herbs.

1/2 cup butter or margarine, melted
2 packages (of 10) flaky biscuits

1/2 teaspoon fine herbs (parsley, chervil, chives, tarragon, oregano, basil, or any of your favorite herbs)

Spray entire Bundt pan with vegetable spray. Pour melted butter in pan and sprinkle with herbs. Stand up biscuits all around pan in a circle, overlapping if possible.

Bake at 375 degrees F for 20 to 25 minutes (while chicken casserole is baking).

Turn out onto serving dish (herbs will be on top). Serve hot. Pull apart to eat.

Note: Fine herbs (a classic herb mix used in France) includes equal parts of parsley, chervil, chives, and tarragon. I often use oregano and basil instead because I like the way they smell.

Succotash   Makes 6 servings

This is also good with baked ham and apple-cheese casserole (p.19). The secret is fresh corn and tiny butter beans. I grew up shucking corn and shelling butter beans on my grandparents' farm in Bulloch County. Believe me, I am happy to pay for this service at the farmers' market. I often use frozen butter beans in this dish, and I can't tell the difference. Be sure to choose the tiniest ones, not those huge lima beans, which are an entirely different vegetable altogether.

2 cups fresh corn, cut from the cob with
   a small knife (about 3 medium ears)
1/2 teaspoon salt
1/2 teaspoon pepper
1/4 teaspoon garlic powder
1 chicken bouillon cube

2 cups tiny butter beans
2 tablespoons butter or margarine
2 tablespoons half-and-half

Remove the corn from the cob by standing the corn up in a large, deep bowl and cutting the kernels from the cob with a small, sharp knife. Set aside.

In a medium saucepan with a lid, combine 2 cups water with butter beans, salt, pepper, garlic powder, and bouillon cube. Bring the water to a rolling boil. Reduce heat, cover, and cook butter beans for 18 minutes. Add the corn and continue to cook for about 5 minutes. Drain off most of the water, leaving about 1/4 cup. Add the butter and the half-and-half. Serve immediately, or refrigerate until you need it.

Reheat in a saucepan over low heat just until hot, or reheat in the microwave on high for 2 minutes, until steaming .

Lime Cheesecake   Serves 12 to 16

This dessert tastes equally good with chicken or seafood dishes.

2 cups graham cracker crumbs

2 1/2 cups sugar, divided

1/2 cup melted butter

4 (8-ounce) packages of cream cheese, softened

5 large eggs

2 teaspoons grated lime rind

1/2 cup fresh lime juice

2 teaspoons vanilla, divided

8 ounces of sour cream

Stir together the crumbs, 1/4 cup of the sugar, and the butter. Press the mixture into the bottom and up the sides as far as it will go (about 1/2 an inch) of a 9-inch springform pan that you have sprayed with vegetable spray. Chill for 1 hour.

Preheat oven to 325 degrees F. Beat the cream cheese until smooth. Add eggs, beating after adding each one. Gradually add 1 3/4 cups sugar, lime rind, juice, and 1 teaspoon of the vanilla. Pour the mixture into the cold crust. Place the springform pan onto a baking sheet, which will help you when it's time to remove the cake. Bake the cake for 1 hour and 15 minutes, until the center is almost set. Combine the remaining 1/2 cup of sugar, 1 teaspoon vanilla, and the sour cream. Spread it evenly over the cake. Bake for 10 minutes more. Remove from the oven, and allow to sit in the pan on the counter for 1 hour.

Wrap well in the springform and chill overnight.

Remove from the refrigerator about 30 minutes before serving. Cut with a large, sharp knife, wiping with a paper towel between cuts if needed.

4th of July Cookout

It is always as hot as blue blazes in the South in July, so why in the world would we go outside to eat? Tradition! Southerners brave the heat and the mosquitoes in honor of our nation's birthday and are determined to dine outdoors on barbecued something—ribs, Boston butts chopped into barbecue, or chicken. And if you want your party to be a success, you start it off with boiled peanuts. We never have a summer family reunion without them.

For this menu, I've chosen some non-traditional accompaniments just because I like them—roasted vegetables tossed with pasta and pesto, cole slaw in a vinaigrette, and rosemary olive bread. But for dessert, I've reverted back to the traditional—sticking with either cherry pie, apple pie, or peach cobbler. The blueberry crumble from the fried fish menu also works with this meal.

Prepare the crab dip, boiled peanuts, barbecue sauce, and rosemary bread a day in advance. The morning of the party, chop the slaw ingredients and all of the vegetables for the grilled vegetable and pasta dish. Prepare the pie or the cobbler, but do not bake until the guests arrive so they can smell the fruit cooking during the party. While guests are nibbling on the crab dip and peanuts, grill the ribs and vegetables as they watch. Or, let them help. You can even toss the pasta at the table in a large bowl. Your cooking show will whet your guests' appetites.

This is a messy meal—the peanuts ooze juice and the ribs are coated with sauce, so have plenty of paper towels on hand. Pass the towelettes before you serve dessert.

Salute to the Military

Savannah has a huge military presence due to Hunter Army Airfield and Fort Stewart, near Hinesville, Georgia. We salute our fine troops and the families who support them.

Crab Dip   Serves 10 to 12

During the summer, Low Country crabbers catch their own blue crab using chicken necks and string—I'm not kidding! Then, they sit around a table and pick the meat from the claws and body cavities until they have enough of the wonderful crabmeat to make a dip like this one.

1 pound of fresh blue crab meat, white or claw, picked through for shells

1 small can of water chestnuts, drained and finely chopped

1/2 cup mayonnaise

3 tablespoons chopped green onion

1 teaspoon soy sauce

Dash of cayenne pepper

Combine the crab meat, water chestnuts, mayonnaise, green onions, soy sauce, and cayenne in a bowl and mix well. Chill, covered, for 2 hours. Serve with melba toast rounds or other favorite crackers.

Cole Slaw with Vinaigrette

This is a nice change from the cole slaw made with mayonnaise.

Balsamic Vinaigrette:

1/4 cup red wine vinegar

1/4 cup balsamic vinegar

1 cup olive oil

1/2 teaspoon Dijon mustard

1/2 teaspoon salt

1/4 teaspoon coarse black pepper

Mixed Vegetable Slaw:

1/2 head each green and red cabbages, shredded

1/2 head Chinese cabbage, shredded

Several bunches of arugula

1/4 cup chives, diced

1/4 cup Vidalia or green onions, diced

Combine dressing ingredients in a small bowl and whisk vigorously until combined. Add about 1/2 cup of the marinade to the slaw just before serving. Taste. Add more marinade if needed.

Barbecued Ribs with Richard's Sauce

There is great debate with ribs—cook them directly over the coals, or cook them indirectly long and slow. This recipe calls for the ribs to be boiled, then briefly grilled.

1 pound of pork spareribs per person
2/3 cup sugar
2 tablespoons pepper
1 teaspoon salt
2 cups red wine vinegar
Basting sauce:
Red wine vinegar
Lots of black pepper

Sauce:
1 (10-ounce) can chicken broth
1 pint apple cider vinegar
1 cup Heinz 57 sauce
1/4 cup Texas Pete hot sauce
1 tablespoon salt
1 tablespoon black pepper
1 teaspoon red pepper
1/2 cup (1 stick) butter
2 cups ketchup

Ribs should be about 3 inches across. If they are larger, have butcher cut them down the middle to make short ribs. Wash ribs. Pat them dry. Combine sugar, pepper, and salt in shaker jar and coat ribs with mixture. Allow to marinate at room temperature about 30 minutes.

Boil ribs in red-wine vinegar and enough water to cover ribs until all fat cooks out, about 30 minutes.

Remove ribs from water. Add more dry marinade from shaker jar. Cook ribs over indirect heat over coals until they develop a smoky flavor, about 30 minutes. Baste with red-wine vinegar and pepper mixture. You may add barbecue sauce the last 15 minutes, basting continuously. Cook ribs over direct heat the last few minutes, to brown.

Cut ribs before serving. Dribble sauce over all. Serve more sauce separately.

If serving ribs with accompaniments, as in this menu, you can reduce the amount of ribs to a half pound per person.

To make the sauce: Combine all ingredients. In a medium saucepan, simmer uncovered for 2 hours. Stir occasionally to keep from sticking. Keep in a quart jar with a screw-on lid.

Grilled Vegetables with Pasta and Pesto   Serves 10 to 12

This is a beautiful dish, using all of the best produce of summer.

1 small eggplant, peeled and julienned

1 small zucchini, peeled and julienned

1 yellow squash, lightly pared and julienned

Red and yellow sweet peppers, julienned

1 large Vidalia (sweet) onion, julienned

Marinade:

1/3 cup olive oil

3 tablespoons lemon juice

1/4 cup chopped onions

1/4 cup chopped fresh basil

2 cloves garlic, minced

3/4 teaspoons salt

1 teaspoon fennel seeds, crushed

Coarsely ground black pepper

12 ounces of bow tie pasta, cooked according to package directions

3 tablespoons pesto

1 (14-ounce) can of diced tomatoes, with juice

1/4 cup Parmesan cheese

2 tablespoons fresh basil, finely chopped

Combine marinade ingredients in a small glass bowl; whisk. Place the vegetables and the marinade in a 1-gallon plastic bag. Marinate for several hours. Drain.

Grill vegetables in grill basket over medium high heat until done to taste—about 15 minutes (I like the vegetables very done, almost charred).

Cook bow tie pasta. Drain. Toss with vegetables, pesto, diced tomatoes, Parmesan cheese, and chopped basil.

Serve warm or at room temperature.

Leftovers are terrific as is, or with boiled shrimp tossed in.

Olive Country Bread with Rosemary Makes 2 loaves

This hearty, beautiful, aromatic bread will impress your guests.

---

1 package dry yeast

1/2 cup warm water

1 1/2 cups warm milk

2 tablespoons sugar

1/2 cup cornmeal, plus extra for baking sheet

3 tablespoons unsalted butter, softened

1 cup coarsely chopped onion

4 tablespoons rosemary, coarsely chopped

2/3 cup pitted Calamata olives, halved

2 teaspoons salt

1 tablespoon coarse ground pepper

2 cups whole wheat flour

3 to 3 1/2 cups unbleached all-purpose flour

Stir yeast, water, milk, and sugar together. Allow to sit until foamy.

Combine cornmeal, butter, onion, rosemary, olives, salt, pepper, whole wheat flour and 2 cups all-purpose flour. Add yeast mixture; beat well. Place dough on floured board and add remaining flour as necessary until dough is workable and non-sticky. Allow dough to rest for 10 to 15 minutes.

Knead until smooth and elastic, adding more flour if necessary to keep from sticking.

Allow dough to rise, covered, in lightly oiled bowl for about 1 1/2 hours. Punch dough down with your fist. Divide in half. Shape into round loaves. Sprinkle baking sheet with a little cornmeal and place loaves on it. Cover with kitchen towel and let rise again, about 45 minutes.

Preheat oven to 350 degrees F. Bake until bread is well browned, about 45 minutes. Remove from baking sheet and set on wire rack to cool.

Loaves freeze well.

Aunt Eunice's Cherry Pie Serves 8

Anne Coakley of Savannah shared this heirloom recipe.

1 (15-ounce) can sour pitted cherries	Crust:
1/4 can water	2 cups all-purpose flour
3/4 cup sugar	1 1/2 teaspoons salt
3 tablespoons tapioca (rounded)	1/2 cup vegetable oil
1 teaspoon vanilla	1/4 cup cold water
Pinch salt	
1/2 cup (1 stick) butter, room temperature	1/4 cup sugar

Combine the cherries, water, sugar, and tapioca in a 1-quart non-stick pot. Cook over medium heat until the mixture is thick and clear, about 3 minutes. Cool. Add vanilla, salt, and butter. Stir well.

To make the crust, combine the flour and salt and stir. Combine the oil and water and make a well in the center of the dry ingredients. Add liquid ingredients and stir. Divide the dough into halves, and roll out between wax paper. Put one half in pie pan by removing the top layer of waxed paper and flipping the pie crust into the pie pan. Carefully remove the waxed paper and press the crust into the pan. Crimp the top edge. Add filling. Cut the other half into strips and lattice over top. Sprinkle 1/4 cup sugar over crust.

Preheat oven to 450 degrees F. Place the pie on a cookie sheet and bake for 10 minutes. Reduce heat to 350 and bake for 30 minutes more. Serve warm or cold.

Boiled Peanuts Serves 10 to 12

At an old-fashioned barbecue in Vidalia, Ga., in 1977, the menu included 60 pounds of smoked Boston butts, chopped and smothered with barbecue sauce; bowls of slaw, 100 ears of freshly picked corn ready for boiling, hundreds of homegrown tomatoes ready for slicing, and, for starters, boiled peanuts. Southerners grow up on boiled peanuts. Beware. You can't eat just a few.

5 pounds raw peanuts	1 cup of salt

Wash raw peanuts thoroughly. Put peanuts in large pot and cover completely with water. Pour salt over top of peanuts. Bring water to a boil, cover the pot but leave the lid so that steam can escape, reduce heat to medium, and boil until peanuts are tender but still firm, about 45 minutes to an hour. Taste periodically (this is the fun part.) If necessary, add more water to keep peanuts covered. When done, turn off the heat and allow the peanuts to sit in the water until they sink—at this point, they have absorbed the salt. Drain. Serve hot, or refrigerate and serve cold.

Apple Pie with Crumb Topping   Serves 8

This all-American dessert is the perfect choice for a July 4th party. Serve warm, topped with whipped cream or vanilla ice cream, if desired.

1 ready-made pie crust	1/2 cup (1 stick) butter, softened
4 to 5 large tart apples	1 cup brown sugar
1/2 cup granulated sugar	1 cup flour
Juice of 1 lemon	1/2 cup chopped pecans or other nuts

Peel and slice apples into pie crust. The crust should be very full. Sprinkle with granulated sugar and lemon juice.

Cream butter and brown sugar. Work in flour and nuts with fork or fingers. Crumble topping over apples. Bake at 300 degrees F for 45 minutes.

· ·

Peach Cobbler   Serves 6 to 8

I've had this recipe since 1984, when it was sent to me by cookbook author Nathalie Dupree. It's best when the peaches are at their peak, in June and July. Serve it warm (yes, even in summer!), with ice cream.

1/2 cup butter	1 cup sugar
1 cup self-rising flour	2 cups sliced fresh peaches, with juice
1 cup milk	Whipped cream or ice cream, to top

Preheat oven to 350 degrees F. Put butter in 13 x 9-inch pan and place the pan in the oven long enough for the butter to melt, about 5 minutes.

While butter is melting, mix well the flour, milk, and sugar.

Pour batter evenly over melted butter. Do not stir. Distribute peaches and juice on top of the batter. Do not stir. Bake for 30 to 35 minutes, until browned. Crust will rise up around peaches.

Simple Fish
Suppers

The one thing that I do well is cook fish. But many of my friends have told me they are afraid to have fish on the menu when they are inviting friends in for supper. Let's change that!

This menu provides you with three fish options. The pan-fried flounder recipe is easy and delicious, and many cooks who have never had good luck with fish have tried it with wonderful results. Thank you, Gerry Klaskala, wherever you are, for teaching me this method for cooking flounder. You can cook other thin fillets, like tilapia and trout, the same way. You will need a large, non-stick, flat-bottomed pan for best results. If your pan is not large enough to hold the fillets, try an electric skillet.

Another fish option is pecan-coated grouper, one of my family's favorites; you can substitute any thick, white fish. However, you will need a frying pan with a metal handle that can go into the oven so that the fish can cook all of the way through. Chefs call this "finishing."

As a third option, I've included a recipe for grilling salmon, salmon being readily available just about everywhere in the United States thanks to flash-freezing. If you know how to light a grill—charcoal or gas—you will like this recipe.

When I am preparing a fish meal, I do everything else in advance as much as possible so that the night of the party, the only thing I have to do is worry about the main course. Completely prepare the lemon souffle, the pesto and tomato terrine, and the green sauce for the fish. Have the cheese biscuits and oven-roasted garlic potatoes ready to go in the oven, and the fish and asparagus ready to go in the pan. The night of the party, you'll only have to put the potatoes and cheese biscuits in the oven (creating a heavenly smell) when the guests arrive. The fish and the asparagus are the two items you'll cook at the last minute, while your guests mingle around you. People love to watch someone else cook.

Before I leave fish dinners, I have to talk about the Southern fish fry. I grew up eating fresh-water fish—bream, catfish, and bass. When we moved to Savannah, my family discovered salt-water fishing, and I learned to fry salt-water fish. We really prefer to fillet the fish and cut it into serving-size pieces—it's just so much nicer not to have to worry about the bones. With fried fish, you just have to serve cheese grits, cole slaw, hush puppies, and blueberry crumble for dessert. Enjoy!

Pesto and Tomato Terrine   Serves 8 to 10

This is particularly nice in summer, but it also makes a festive holiday hors d'oeuvre because of the red, green and white layers.

1/2 cup (1 stick) softened butter

8 ounces softened cream cheese

2 tablespoons basil pesto

2 tablespoons sun-dried tomato pesto

Mix butter and cream cheese with a mixer in a medium bowl until well-combined. Line a small glass bowl with plastic wrap, leaving lots of overhang. Using a spatula, place half of the butter-cream cheese mixture in the bottom of the bowl, smoothing the top so that it is flat. Carefully spread a layer of the basil pesto over the cream cheese. Then add the layer of sun-dried tomato pesto. Take the remaining half of the cream-cheese mixture and spread it on top of the tomato pesto. Cover the cream cheese with the plastic wrap overhang. Refrigerate.

When ready to serve, unwrap the top of the mold and invert it onto a plate. Remove plastic wrap. Serve at room temperature with bland crackers.

Pan-Fried Flounder Serves 4 to 6

When I was a new food editor at the Savannah Morning News, *the chef at the Hyatt, Gerry Klaskala, took me into the kitchen and taught me how to cook fish. Thanks, Gerry!*

---

4 (8-ounce) flounder fillets, with skin on one side (you may use other thin fish fillets, such as tilapia)
Salt and pepper to taste
1/2 cup all-purpose flour, for dredging
2 tablespoons vegetable oil, such as canola

3 tablespoons butter, divided
Juice of 1 lemon
1 (2 or 3-ounce) bottle of capers, with juice

Wash fillets in cold water and pat dry. Salt and pepper rather heavily. Place the flour in a plastic bag and dredge fish in flour. Place the oil and 2 tablespoons of butter in a flat, heavy-bottomed skillet and heat on medium-high until butter melts. Keeping heat at medium-high, cook fish on one side 3 to 5 minutes, depending on size of fillets, until deep brown and crispy. Turn fish and cook on second side 3 to 5 minutes, until deep brown and crispy. Turn fish only once.

Remove fish to serving platter.

Turn off heat. Into hot skillet, whisk in additional tablespoon of butter. Add lemon juice. Pour in capers, juice and all. Whisk until blended. Pour thin sauce over fish fillets. Serve at once.

Serves 4 to 6, depending on size of fillets. Serve half or third portions of fish to each guest.

Note: Flounder fillets come in all sizes. You will have to eyeball what is available to determine how many you will need to feed the guests you have. Generally, allow 6 to 8 ounces of fish per person.

Pecan-Coated Grouper Serves 4

I first had pecan-coated snapper at a black-tie event, then pecan-coated rainbow trout years later at the Brasstown Ball lodge in north Georgia. Pecan coating works as well with grouper as it does snapper and rainbow trout. The secret is to cook the fish through, without burning the pecans.

4 (4 ounce) grouper fillets, (a good fish
   market will cut these for you)
1/2 cup melted butter for coating fillets
Salt and pepper
1 tablespoon butter, for cooking fish

1 tablespoon oil
1 cup pecans, minced into crumbs in
   food processor (be sure not to make
    into pecan butter!)

Preheat oven to 350 degrees F.

Wash fillets in cold water and pat dry. Lightly salt and pepper fillets. Roll each fillet in butter, then press into pecans to coat each side. Place butter and oil into a heavy, oven-proof skillet and heat until butter melts and pan is hot. Sear fish on both sides in skillet, about 2 minutes each side. Be careful not to burn nuts. Place the fish in the skillet into the oven and cook fish 8 to 10 minutes, depending on the thickness of the fish. For 8 guests, prepare eight fillets in two skillets.

Serve immediately with Green Sauce.

Teriyaki Grilled Salmon Serves 6

This is terrific hot, but I adore it the next day, cold with the green sauce. I always prepare an extra fillet or two so that I have leftovers.

6 (4 to 6-ounce) salmon fillets	1/4 cup pineapple juice
Butter	1/4 cup brown sugar
Salt and pepper	2 cloves of garlic, minced
	1 tablespoon sherry
Marinade:	
1/2 cup teriyaki sauce	

Wash fillets in cold water and pat dry. Combine marinade ingredients in a resealable freezer bag and place the salmon in the bag. Refrigerate overnight, or marinate at room temperature for at least 30 minutes.

Take heavy-duty aluminum foil and create several small trays by turning up the four sides. Brush the foil with butter, then salt and pepper liberally. Remove the salmon from the marinade and place skin side down onto the foil. Place the foil trays on a hot grill, place the cover on the grill, and allow the fish to cook for 12 minutes. Check several times to make sure the grill is not too hot and the fish is not burning. Serve immediately with Green Sauce.

• •

Green Sauce Makes about 1 1/2 cups

This is great with either the pecan grouper or the salmon. It's not bad on the hot asparagus!

1 cup chopped parsley	2/3 cup mayonnaise
1/4 cup chopped green onion	1 tablespoon olive oil
1 tablespoon capers	1 tablespoon lemon juice
1 clove minced garlic	1/2 teaspoon prepared mustard

Combine parsley, green onion, capers, and garlic in blender or food processor. Add mayonnaise, olive oil, lemon juice, and mustard. Blend. Chill. Serve with fish or oysters.

Asparagus With Lemon Butter Serves 6 to 8

I have prepared this dozens of times—at bridal showers, prom dinners, and family suppers. It's the perfect accent to fish.

1 pound fresh asparagus, thin
  stalks preferred
4 tablespoons butter
Juice of 1 lemon

Wash asparagus. Line asparagus up on a cutting board with tops even. Cut off tough ends of bottoms, as much as 1 1/2 inches. If stalks are thin and tender, it is not necessary to peel them. If stalks are large, peel them lightly with a vegetable peeler.

Bring a skillet or oval casserole filled half full of salted water to boil. Dump in asparagus all at once. When water returns to the boil, cook asparagus from 1 to 5 minutes, depending on its size and your preference.

Immediately drain. Add butter and lemon juice to hot skillet and whisk. Return the asparagus to the skillet. Use tongs to turn asparagus so that all stalks are coated with sauce.

Or, prepare in advance, refrigerate in clean, damp towels and reheat by dumping briefly into boiling water. Asparagus can also be served cold, with vinaigrette, but not with butter sauce.

Kacey's Cheese Biscuits Makes about 40 biscuits

Kacey was my neighbor and she prepared these for her daughter's christening lunch. My sons love them, and it's nice to have a pan in the oven when they walk through the door. The aroma says, "Welcome home."

3/4 cup butter, room temperature
1 1/2 cups grated sharp Cheddar cheese
1/4 cup Parmesan cheese

1/2 teaspoon salt
1 ½ cups all-purpose flour

In food processor, cream butter and cheeses. Sift together salt and flour. Add to butter-cheese mixture. Pulse processor. Blend just until mixture forms a ball. Mixture will be soft. Spoon out evenly onto two pieces of waxed paper and wrap paper around cheese, forming with hands into a long roll about the diameter of a silver dollar. Refrigerate until firm. Slice into 1/2 -inch thick slices on unbuttered non-stick cookie sheets. Bake at 350 degrees F for 12 to 15 minutes.
   Dough freezes well.

Hot Dip for Chicken or Fish Makes 1 1/2 cups

This dip is a gorgeous salmon color and has a terrific flavor, but watch out—it's hot!

1 cup mayonnaise
8 ounces cream cheese, softened

1/4 cup pickled jalapeno peppers,
   diced
1 (2-ounce) jar pimientos, diced

Combine the mayonnaise and cream cheese in a medium bowl with snap-on lid. Mix well. Add jalapenos and pimiento and mix. Keep refrigerated until ready to use. Remove from refrigerator 30 minutes before serving so that cream cheese can soften.

Cold Lemon Souffle with Wine Sauce Serves 8

I ran across this recipe thirty years ago and thought it was the most wonderful summer dessert ever created. When my husband and I participated in the 1984 March of Dimes Gourmet Gala, this was the dish we chose to prepare...and it won top prize! After it was printed in the newspaper, several readers called to say that they had adopted it as their standard dinner party dessert. The secret is the healthy dose of fresh lemon juice and lemon rind.

1 envelope unflavored gelatin	**Wine Sauce:**
1/4 cup cold water	1/2 cup sugar
5 eggs, separated	1 tablespoon cornstarch
3/4 cup fresh lemon juice	1/2 cup water
1 tablespoon grated lemon rind	3 tablespoons fresh lemon juice
1 1/4 cups sugar	2 teaspoons grated lemon rind
1 cup whipping cream	2 tablespoons butter
	1/4 cup dry white wine
Blueberries, for garnish	

Mix gelatin in cold water to soften. Combine egg yolks, lemon juice, rind, and sugar in saucepan. Cook over low heat, stirring constantly, until mixture is slightly thickened, about 8 minutes. Remove from heat and stir in gelatin mixture until completely dissolved. Chill about 20 minutes.

Beat egg whites; fold into lemon mixture. Whip cream; fold into lemon mixture.

Pour into 2-quart souffle dish and chill at least four hours.

Serve with wine sauce. To make wine sauce: In a small saucepan, mix sugar and cornstarch; add water, lemon juice, and rind. Stir until smooth. Add butter. Bring to a boil, lower heat and cook until thickened (happens very quickly). Remove from heat. Stir in wine. Chill. Stir before serving.

Serve several scoops of souffle with a tablespoon of wine sauce and fresh blueberries.

Fried Fish

Use any kind of fish fillets - bass, trout, king mackerel steaks, etc. (Allow 1 or 2 fillets per person; or, with small fish with bone in, such as bream or mullet, allow 3 fish per person.)

1 cup cornmeal
1/2 cup all-purpose flour
Salt and pepper
Oil for frying fish

Place cornmeal and flour in paper bag. Season with salt and pepper and shake well. Toss in several fish at a time and shake bag to coat fish with cornmeal mixture. Fish can be cooked indoors in a large, deep frying pan in about 3 inches of oil. (Warning: The smell of fried fish lingers!) Or, for large crowds, it is best to cook fish in a gallon of oil in a cast-iron fish cooker outside. Cook fish in hot oil until they are browned on all sides; time varies according to thickness of fish.

As each batch is completed, place fish on baking sheets lined with brown paper, and place in a 200 degree F oven to keep warm until all are ready and can be served.

Eloise's Tarter Sauce Makes 2 1/2 cups

Eloise Wardell makes the best tarter sauce. It also goes well with crab cakes.

4 tablespoons finely minced onion
2 cups mayonnaise
1/2 cup sweet pickle relish

1 tablespoon dried parsley flakes
1 1/2 teaspoons dried dill weed
1/2 teaspoon Nature's Seasons

Combine ingredients. Mix well. Cover and refrigerate. Keeps three weeks in refrigerator.

Baked Garlic Cheese Grits   Serves 8 to 10

I've been making these since I moved to Savannah. Baking the grits keeps the texture consistent.

1 cup regular grits, uncooked	1 tablespoon Worcestershire sauce
4 cups water	Dash of hot sauce (optional)
1 teaspoon salt	8 ounces grated sharp Cheddar cheese
1/2 cup butter or margarine	2 eggs, lightly beaten
1 garlic clove, minced or pressed	

Preheat oven to 350 degrees F. Cook grits according to package directions in salted water. Add butter, garlic, Worcestershire sauce, hot sauce (if using) and Cheddar cheese. Add a small amount of hot grits to eggs to temper them, then add eggs to rest of grits. Stir well.

Pour mixture into buttered, 2-quart casserole and bake 45 to 50 minutes, until set. If desired, top casserole with thin cheese slices in pattern, which will melt in the last few minutes of cooking.

Serves 8 to 10 as side dish.

•••

Sweet Tea   Makes 1 1/2 quarts

You will see sweet tea on most of our menus. The hotter is gets, the sweeter Southerners like their tea!

2 family-sized tea bags
1 cup sugar

Bring 1 quart of water to boil. Place tea bags in water, turn off heat, and allow tea to steep for 20 minutes. Pour warm tea into a pitcher and stir in sugar until sugar dissolves. Add 2 more cups of water and chill before serving.

Hush Puppies Makes 2 dozen

No good Southern fish fry is complete without hush puppies.

Cornmeal used to batter fish
1 additional cup self-rising
  cornmeal mix
1/2 cup finely chopped onion

1 egg
Beer (or water) enough to make thick
  but smooth consistency (about 1/2 to
  2/3 cup)

Combine ingredients and stir well. Allow batter to sit for 10 minutes; it should be the consistency of mush. Spoon by teaspoonfuls into hot fish grease and fry until hush puppies float and are brown on all sides, about 5 minutes.

· ·

Blueberry Crumble Serves 4

This might be the easiest dessert recipe in the cookbook. It takes ten minutes to put together, and it's just delicious. It's terrific hot with whipped cream or vanilla ice cream. You can easily double the recipe if you're serving eight guests. Savannah cook Patty Ronning shared this recipe.

1 pint blueberries
2 tablespoons lemon juice
1/3 cup sugar

Topping:
3/4 cup all-purpose flour
1/4 teaspoon salt
1/3 cup sugar
1/3 cup butter, at room temperature

Preheat oven to 350 degrees F. Combine blueberries, lemon juice, and sugar. Place in 1-quart casserole sprayed with vegetable spray. Combine flour, salt, and sugar. Cut in margarine to make crumbly topping. Crumble evenly over top of blueberries. Bake for 30 minutes, until berries are syrupy and topping is lightly browned.

Lemon Meringue Pie Serves 8

This recipe was given to be by a wonderful cook, now long gone. This is a classic Southern dessert. When you can make a perfect lemon meringue pie, you are a GOOD COOK.

1 1/2 cups sugar

1/2 cup cornstarch

1/4 teaspoon salt

1 1/2 cups cold water

3 large lemons, juiced

5 egg yolks

2 tablespoons butter

3 teaspoons grated lemon rind

1 (8-ounce) can crushed pineapple, drained (optional)

1 deep-dish pie shell, baked

Meringue:

5 egg whites

1/4 teaspoon cream of tartar

1/2 cup sugar

1/2 teaspoon vanilla

To make the filling, mix sugar, cornstarch, and salt in saucepan. Add water and juice from lemons and cook over medium heat until mixture is very warm, stirring constantly. Remove 1 cup of warm mixture and add to beaten egg yolks. Return mixture to saucepan. Cook until very thick. Remove from heat. Add butter and stir until melted. Add lemon rind, and pineapple, if using. Pour warm mixture into warm pie shell. Top with meringue.

To make the meringue: Beat egg whites, adding cream of tartar slowly. Beat until foamy. Slowly add sugar, beating until stiff. Add vanilla. Spread meringue over filling, taking care to seal edges of meringue to all edges of crust.

  Bake meringue-topped pie for 12 minutes at 350 degrees F. Allow to sit at room temperature. Serve same day for best results.

Low Country Boil

When I was a very young food writer for the *Savannah Morning News*, I interviewed Franc White, whose show, "Southern Sportsman," came on television on Saturday nights at 11:30 p.m.. He taught me to make what he called a Frogmore Stew, which I later learned is also called Low Country Boil. No matter what you call it, it has to be just about the easiest way to entertain there is. You literally put the ingredients—sausage, new potatoes, corn on the cob, and large shrimp—into a large pot, boil them until done, and dump them into a large bowl or even onto newspaper lined tables outdoors. Serve with a salad and plenty of sauces.

However, don't be fooled into thinking there isn't an art to this dish. Each ingredient has to be added to the pot at precisely the right moment, or you'll end up with mush. The trick is to get the water seasoned with the yummy sausage, the potatoes, and corn cooked to perfection, and the shrimp firm in the middle but not overcooked. When my college sons are home, we throw in king crab legs for a few minutes before adding the shrimp. This takes the dish over the top. At least, that's what they tell me.

Tips

Two days before the party: make Pecan Tassies; refrigerate in tins.

Buy groceries. Make salad dressing.

One day before the party: buy the ingredients for the Low Country Boil.

Morning of the party: make cocktail sauce and tartar sauce.

Cut salad ingredients—store each ingredient individually in plastic bags in refrigerator.

Cut sausage and clean corn during the party. Once the sausage is in the water, wash, trim and quarter the new potatoes—add to the pot when needed.

Toss the salad when you add the corn to the pot.

Put bread in oven if serving.

Have on hand: hot pads, large strainers, bowls for condiments, large bowl to toss the salad, and large serving platter.

Burma Bomb

This drink is a refreshing way to wile away a hot summer afternoon while watching dolphins from a neighbor's dock. Leave the recipe by the bar with all of the ingredients, and let each guest make their own. This recipe comes from caterer Trish McLeod.

Per Drink:

1 1/2 ounces Bacardi Gold Rum (Ronrico)

6 ounces Fresca, ginger ale or tonic

2-3 splashes pink grapefruit juice
cocktail or orange juice

Sprigs of mint

Combine liquid ingredients. Serve over ice with sprigs of mint as garnish.

Spinach Salad Serves 6 to 8

The tanginess of this salad will complement the seafood in this menu.

Salad:

10 ounces baby spinach, washed and
  dried, stems removed

4 strips bacon, fried crisp and
  crumbled

2 hard-cooked eggs, chopped

1 cup sliced fresh mushrooms

2 green onions, sliced

6 cherry tomatoes, halved
  (or 2 regular tomatoes, cut in eighths)

Dressing:

1 cup vegetable oil

1/4 cup red wine vinegar

1/4 cup fresh lemon juice

1 teaspoon salt

1/2 teaspoon pepper

3 teaspoons sugar

1 teaspoon dry mustard

1 garlic clove, minced

In a large salad bowl, place spinach, bacon, eggs, mushrooms, green onions, and tomatoes. Cover with plastic wrap and refrigerate. Combine dressing ingredients in a jar with tight lid; shake well. Immediately before serving, add dressing. Toss salad well.

Low Country Boil   Serves 8

Cooks often add ingredients to Low Country Boil—Vidalia onions, chunks of carrot, even arti-chokes! However, I just like the basic variety. Sometimes I add the Old Bay seasoning, and sometimes I don't. The sausage is what really seasons the water.

2 pounds kielbasa Polish sausage,
  sliced into 2-inch pieces
1/4 cup Old Bay Seasoning (optional)
24 new potatoes, halved or quartered,
  depending on size

4 to 6 ears corn, broken in half
3 pounds large shrimp

Condiments:
Soft butter, sour cream, sliced lemons

Allow 1 hour to heat water in 20-gallon pot, filled about one-third full. Add Old Bay, if using. About 45 minutes before serving, add sausage. About 20 minutes before serving, add new potatoes. Add corn about 15 minutes before serving. If using King Crab clusters, add them about 10 minutes before serving. About 5 minutes before serving, add shrimp. When shrimp turn pink and are cooked through (5 minutes or less), drain contents. Serve hot.

   Note: Test a shrimp from the bottom of the pot about 3 minutes after you add the shrimp.

   Have soft butter and sour cream available for corn and potatoes, and sliced lemons for squeezing.

· ·

Horseradish Cocktail Sauce

This is a "must" when serving Low Country Boil.

2 cups ketchup
2 teaspoons horseradish
Juice of 1 lemon

Combine. Chill. Serve. (For Eloise's Tartar Sauce, see page 135.)

Garlic Bread Serves 8

> 1 large loaf Italian or French bread
> 1/2 cup butter, left out overnight
>
> 2 cloves garlic, minced

Combine the softened butter and garlic in a small dish. Cover until ready to use. Slice bread into 1 1/2-inch thick slices. Bring butter to room temperature, spread on slices, and toast in 350-degree F oven for about 5 to 7 minutes, until lightly browned.

Pecan Tassies Makes 24

These taste like little pecan pies. They are a standard at Savannah parties, partly because they hold up so well in Savannah's heat and humidity.

> Pastry:
> 3 ounces softened cream cheese
> 1/2 cup softened butter or margarine
> 1 cup all-purpose flour
> 1/4 teaspoon salt
>
> Filling:
> 1 egg, beaten
> 3/4 cup brown sugar
> 2 tablespoons softened butter
> 1/4 teaspoon salt
> 1 teaspoon vanilla
> 1 cup chopped pecans

Mix pastry ingredients until blended. Chill. Form pastry into 24 balls; press with hands into bottom and up sides of ungreased miniature muffin tins.

For filling, beat together all ingredients except pecans.

Sprinkle a few nuts in the bottom of each pastry shell. Pour filling over nuts, filling each tin 3/4 full.

Bake at 350 degrees F for 20-25 minutes, or until filling is set.

Cool slightly; remove from muffin tins by running knife around edges. Cool on wire racks. Store in tightly covered container.

Wild Game
Dinner

Southerners have a long tradition of hunting and feasting on wild game. This menu is for those who hunt and those who just enjoy the idea of eating game. It features quail, dove, and venison tenderloin. Because wild game typically has such a strong taste, you need side dishes that can hold their own—Brussels sprouts, wild rice, and an apple cake fit the bill.

In my previous cookbook, "Savannah Entertains," a hunting friend explained the attraction Southerners feel to the land. "Hunting is a tradition in the Low Country that has often been passed from father to son or daughter. It is a way of life, and the traditions have survived to this day. There is something special about seeing the sun rise or set as you watch an incoming flight of ducks or a svelte deer creeping through the woods. The dawn breaks away from the darkness and in the stillness and the cool of the morning, life begins to erupt around you. With a friend or dog beside you, you watch and wait for the game to come."

Tips

Prepare the apple cake, the quail terrine, and the green sauce two days in advance.

Make the Sally Lunn a day ahead and reheat right before serving.

The wild rice, Brussels sprouts, and curried fruit can cook while the meat is grilling.

Smoked Dove Breasts with Plum Sauce

These smell delicious during grilling.

Juice of 1 lemon

1/4 cup butter, melted

1 teaspoon lemon pepper

1/2 cup Italian dressing

2 teaspoons Worcestershire sauce

12 dove breasts

12 strips of bacon

Plum Sauce:

1 cup plum preserves or plum conserve

1 cup orange juice

Squirt of lemon juice

Mix first five ingredients together in a small dish. Whisk. Place in a plastic bag and add doves; marinate for 1 hour. Wrap each dove with bacon. Spoon marinade mixture over and smoke according to your smoker's directions. Or, bake in 350 degree F oven for 30 to 40 minutes. Juice should run clear when dove is punctured with toothpick. Cut dove into bite-sized pieces.

Spear each with toothpicks. Serve on platter with plum sauce.

To make the plum sauce: Mix all ingredients and simmer until thick. Serve warm as dip with smoked doves.

· ·

Sautéed Brussels Sprouts   Serves 8

32 Brussels sprouts

1/2 cup (1 stick) butter

Salt and pepper to taste

Wash and trim Brussels sprouts. With a knife, cut a 1/2-inch crease into the bottom of each sprout. Boil in 2 cups salted water until just tender, about 7 minutes. Drain and refrigerate until ready to serve. When ready to serve, melt butter in a large saucepan. Add Brussels sprouts and toss in butter until they are warmed and coated. Pepper to taste.

Grilled Venison Tenderloin with Mushroom Sauce Serves 8 to 10

Tenderloin must not be overcooked, or it will become tough and chewy.

1 tenderloin of venison, well-trimmed
2 tablespoons soy sauce
2 tablespoons Kitchen Bouquet
2 tablespoons Worcestershire sauce

Mushroom Sauce:
4 tablespoons butter
6 green onions, mostly green tops
1/2 teaspoon freshly ground pepper
1/2 teaspoon dried thyme
3/4 cup good red table wine

1 pound fresh mushrooms, mixed
  variety—portabellas, button, porcini
1/4 cup flour
2 cups beef stock
2 tablespoons sherry
2 tablespoons brandy
Salt to taste

Combine soy sauce, Kitchen Bouquet, and Worcestershire sauce. Marinate venison tenderloin several hours in a plastic resealable bag. Wrap venison well with bacon, securing with wooden toothpicks. Cook over a hot grill for 15 minutes, turning to cook evenly. Allow to stand about 15 minutes before slicing thin.

To make the sauce: Sauté onions, pepper, and thyme in butter. When vegetables are limp, add red wine. Cook down a little. In a cup or small bowl, make a thick paste with flour and a little beef broth. Add this paste and rest of beef stock to wine mixture. Stir, add sliced mushrooms, sherry, and brandy. Simmer until mushrooms are cooked to your pleasure and sauce is thick.
  Serve with venison tenderloin.

Sally Lunn   Serves 10 to 12

This sweet yeast bread was named for the 18th century Englishwoman from Bath who is said to have first created it in a small bakery for English tea parties. It is most impressive baked in a Bundt pan, sliced and served to guests on a silver platter.

1 package dry yeast	1 1/2 teaspoons salt
1 1/2 cups warm milk	5 cups flour
3 eggs	1/2 cup (1 stick) melted butter
3 tablespoons sugar	

Soften yeast in warm milk in large mixing bowl. In an electric mixer, combine yeast, eggs, and sugar. Add salt and about 3 cups of flour. Stir in remaining flour by hand. Add butter and beat again. Batter will be thin. Let rise in mixing bowl until doubled in bulk, about 1 hour.

Beat down with a wooden spoon and pour into well-greased tube pan or Bundt pan. Let rise again until doubled in bulk, about 1 hour. Bake at 350 degrees F for 45 minutes.

Quail (or Chicken) Terrine
with Green Mayonnaise Serves 8 to 10

Of course, you wouldn't serve chicken at a wild game dinner, but this recipe is delicious when made with chicken. When you slice it, the colors are just beautiful.

8 quail breasts, boned, or 3 chicken
   breasts
2 eggs, slightly beaten
1/2 teaspoon lemon pepper
1/2 teaspoon seasoned salt
1 cup grated Parmesan cheese
8 slices prosciutto
20 large fresh basil leaves
2 (14 1/2-ounce) cans artichoke hearts,
   drained and cut in half

Green Mayonnaise:
1/2 clove garlic
4 tablespoons fresh dill
4 tablespoons fresh chives
   or 1/2 cup fresh dill and no chives
1 tablespoon pasteurized egg product
1/2 teaspoon salt
1 teaspoon dry mustard
2 tablespoons wine vinegar
1 cup vegetable oil

Preheat oven to 350 degrees F. Line a loaf pan with parchment paper. Set aside. Beat eggs and seasonings together. Dip quail breasts and artichoke hearts into egg mixture and coat with Parmesan cheese.

Layer the bottom of a large loaf pan with quail or chicken, cutting pieces to fit, if necessary. Cover the quail or chicken with slices of prosciutto. Cover prosciutto with artichoke hearts. Cover artichoke hearts with basil leaves. Repeat layers of quail and prosciutto, ending with artichoke hearts. Cover the top with parchment paper and weight the top with baking weights or a clean brick. Place loaf pan in a large pan filled with 1 1/2 inches of water. Bake for 1 hour and 20 minutes. Cool completely at room temperature. Refrigerate loaf pan overnight. To serve, carefully remove terrine from pan, remove parchment, and slice into servings, about 1/4 to ½ inch thick. Serve as a first course on a bed of radicchio with rings of yellow and red peppers and green mayonnaise. Or, slice thinly and serve on pumpernickel bread as an hors d'oeuvre.

To make the green mayonnaise: Place all ingredients except the oil in processor. Puree for a second. Add oil in steady stream until emulsified. Note: Pasteurized egg product replaces raw egg to reduce risk of salmonella.

This sauce is also excellent with seafood, or over steamed vegetables.

Hot Curried Fruit   Serves 8

Curried fruit goes great with this meal, but also is a good choice for the holiday office buffet.

1 (15-ounce) can apricot halves	1/2 cup (1 stick) cup butter
1 (15-ounce) can peach halves	3/4 cup brown sugar
1 (15-ounce) can pineapple chunks	2 teaspoons curry powder

Preheat oven to 350 degrees F. Drain fruit in colander. Melt butter in a small saucepan or in a measuring cup in the microwave for one minute on high. And add brown sugar and curry. Place fruit in 2-quart glass baking dish and pour curry sauce evenly over fruit. Bake uncovered for 45 minutes.

Wild Rice with Pecans   Serves 8

1 cup raw wild rice	1/4 cup green onions, sliced
1/4 cup butter or margarine	1/4 cup chopped pecans, toasted
2 1/2 cups chicken stock	

Wash wild rice well. In saucepan, melt butter. Sauté wild rice for a minute in butter. Add chicken stock. Bring rice to a boil, reduce heat to low and cook until rice is tender, about 45-50 minutes. Just before serving, stir in green onions and toasted pecans.

To toast pecans, place chopped nuts in single layer on baking sheet. Toast in 350-degree F oven for about 5 minutes, until they are beginning to brown, but do not burn.

Almond Cookies   Makes 25 cookies

These are a light alternative for dessert.

1/2 cup butter, room temperature

1 1/2 cups powdered sugar

2 teaspoons baking soda

1/4 teaspoon baking powder

Pinch salt

1 teaspoon water

1 egg

1 teaspoon almond extract

2 1/4 cups all-purpose flour

25 almonds

Egg Wash:

1 egg yolk, mixed with 1 teaspoon water

Cream together butter and sugar. Add baking soda, baking powder, salt, water, egg, and almond extract and beat until well mixed. Add flour. Mix together with fork or fingers to form dough.

Pinch off dough and roll into about 25 balls. Place on lightly greased cookie sheet 2 inches apart. Flatten each dough ball with heel of hand. Place an almond in center of each cookie.

Brush egg wash lightly across cookie, almond and dough.

Preheat oven to 350 degrees F. Bake almond cookies for 13 to 15 minutes, until they are a deep yellow color. Do not overbake. Cool on rack. Store in tightly covered container with waxed paper between each layer of cookies.

Fresh Apple Cake   Serves 12 to 16

This cake is moist and delicious, perfect for this meal or with turkey at Thanksgiving. A warning, though: it is crumbly. Serve with plates and forks.

1 1/2 cups vegetable oil

2 cups sugar

3 eggs

3 cups all-purpose flour

1 teaspoon salt

1 teaspoon baking soda

2 teaspoons vanilla

3 freshly chopped apples, Fuji or
   Granny Smith

1 cup chopped pecans

Topping:

1/2 cup butter

1/4 cup evaporated milk

1 cup light brown sugar

1 teaspoon vanilla extract

Whipped cream, for garnish

Preheat oven to 325 degrees F. With electric mixer, combine oil and sugar until light and fluffy. Add slightly beaten eggs. Beat well. Sift together flour, salt, and soda. Add flour mixture to oil mixture. Batter will be very thick. Add vanilla, chopped apples, and pecans. Mix well by hand.

Pour batter into a Bundt pan sprayed with vegetable spray and dusted with flour. Tap cake pan on the counter to remove air pockets. Bake for about 1 1/2 hours, until sides of cake pull away from the pan and a tester inserted into center of cake comes out clean.

Allow cake to cool for 10 minutes in the pan, then invert onto wire rack to cool for additional 15 minutes.

While cake is cooling, make topping. Boil butter, milk, and brown sugar in a saucepan over medium heat for 5 minutes. Add vanilla. Pour warm filling over the top and sides of the cake.

Cake is best made one day in advance so filling can seep into cake. Serve with whipped cream.

Ginger Ice Cream Makes 8 servings

2 cups whole milk	1 cup sugar
2 cups whipping cream	3 beaten egg yolks
5 slices fresh ginger, each about the size of a quarter	2 tablespoons chopped ginger in syrup
	3 tablespoons ginger syrup

Combine milk, cream, and ginger slices; heat to just bubbling over low heat. When bubbles appear on edges, add sugar and stir well. When sugar is completely dissolved, whisk beaten egg yolks into mixture and whisk until incorporated. Keep cooking over low heat until egg yolks are thoroughly cooked, about 8 minutes.

Pour mixture into large glass or stainless steel bowl. Place plastic film over bowl and refrigerate for at least 6 hours.

When ready to make ice cream, remove ginger slices and add chopped stem ginger and ginger syrup. Place mixture in batches in blender or food processor and process until thoroughly mixed.

Make ice cream by churn freezer or electric ice cream mixer, according to directions.

Holiday Office Buffet

Sharing a meal with your colleagues is a way to build community at work. At the charter school where I serve as director of instruction, we have often had covered dish luncheons where the pressures of school melt away. As a "thank you for your business" gesture, I also have prepared buffets for my husband's medical billing clients and office staff. From the feedback that I get, cooking for others seems to be a welcomed holiday gift!

My tips: Think the meal through from beginning to end—do you have all of the essentials—plates or bowls for every dish? Eating and serving utensils? Beverages? Napkins? Platters and bowls for serving? (I love wooden bowls, which don't break and clean up easily.) Ice? Trash bags for disposing of plates, etc.? Plastic bags for sending home leftovers?

In this chapter, I've included some of my most successful dishes, those that have been requested time and time again. You can go as simple as one main dish, one salad, and one dessert … or you can assign your colleagues to each bring an assigned dish and put on the dog. Be sure to have at least one delicious dish for vegetarians; I am finding more and more people who are no longer eating meat.

Figuring out how much of one item to prepare is always a bit tricky. Usually, items go further on a buffet than they do when they are being served as a main course at dinner. Guests usually take a half-cup scoop of each dish; you can add up how many cups are in the casserole and judge accordingly. For example, a casserole that serves six at home might serve 10 to 12 at a buffet.

Also, with this meal, you'll have to think about refrigerator space at the office, and whether your dish will need to be reheated. If you have an oven at the office, you're all set—each casserole should have a sticky note with the time and temperature for baking. Otherwise, microwave ovens, crock pots, and insulated casserole holders all are helpful.

Cranberry Mull Makes 18 (6-ounce) servings

I keep a large percolator at work just for this beverage, which smells delicious and tastes yummy. The pot, however, won't be much good for coffee afterward, as the clove flavor lingers.

1 1/2 quarts cranberry juice

2 quarts apple juice

1/4 cup brown sugar

3 cinnamon sticks

1 tablespoon whole cloves

Additional cinnamon sticks, if desired

Put brown sugar, cinnamon sticks, and cloves in the upper basket of percolator. Pour juices in the bottom of the percolator in place of water. Let mixture perk as if making coffee. Serve with cinnamon sticks as stirrers, if desired.

Squash Casserole Serves 6-8

2 pounds yellow squash, gently pared
  and sliced 1/4 inch thick

1/2 cup chopped onion

1/2 cup (1 stick) butter, divided

2 eggs, beaten

1 1/2 cups grated Cheddar cheese

1/2 cup mayonnaise

8 Saltine crackers, crumbled, divided

1/2 teaspoon salt

1/4 teaspoon pepper

Place squash in a 2-quart pot and add 2 cups water and 1 teaspoon salt. Cook with onion over medium heat, covered, until they are tender, about 10 minutes. Drain. Mash squash and onion with a potato masher. Add 6 tablespoons butter and beaten eggs. Mix well. Add ¾ cup cheese, mayonnaise, and half of the cracker crumbs. Season with salt and pepper.

Place in lightly greased 2-quart casserole. Combine remaining 3/4 cup cheese, and cracker crumbs; top casserole with mixture. Drizzle 2 tablespoons melted butter over topping. Cover and refrigerate.

When ready to bake, preheat oven to 300 degrees F. Bake casserole, uncovered, for 45 minutes, or until puffed, browned, and hot. Note: Freezes well.

Chicken Divan Serves 6 to 8

Of all the casserole-type dishes that I've served over the years, this is one of the most popular. It's also very festive, with the bright green of the broccoli showing through the pale yellow curry sauce.

4 large chicken breast halves, cooked, boned, and torn into bite-sized pieces

2 (10-ounce) packages frozen broccoli, chopped

2 (10 3/4-ounce) cans cream of mushroom soup

3/4 cup mayonnaise

1 (8-ounce) carton sour cream

1 1/2 cups grated sharp Cheddar cheese

1 tablespoon lemon juice

1 1/2 teaspoons curry powder

1/2 teaspoon salt

1/4 teaspoon pepper

3/4 cup dry white wine

Topping:

1/2 cup Parmesan cheese

1/2 cup soft bread crumbs

Or

1 1/2 cups crushed cheese crackers, such as Cheez-Its

3 tablespoons melted butter

Sprinkling of paprika

In a medium saucepan, cook broccoli in 1/2 cup of salted water until hot, about 5 minutes. Drain. Mix together the soup, mayonnaise, sour cream, grated cheese, lemon juice, curry powder, salt, pepper, and wine in a large bowl. Stir well.

Spread shredded chicken in bottom of 13 x 9-inch casserole dish that you have sprayed with vegetable cooking spray. Cover with broccoli. Pour soup mixture over top of broccoli. Spread evenly to cover all of the broccoli. Or, combine chicken, broccoli, and soup mixture, mix well, and spread evenly in a 13 x 9-inch casserole dish. (I love it both ways!)

Combine Parmesan cheese and bread crumbs and sprinkle over top of casserole. Or, top with cheese cracker crumbs. Spoon melted butter over the toppings. Cover and refrigerate.

Preheat oven to 350 degrees F. An hour before serving, remove casserole from refrigerator and allow to sit out, covered, for 30 minutes. Bake uncovered for 30 minutes, until hot and bubbly.

Note: Freezes well.

Aunt Sue's Crab Casserole <small>Serves 6-8</small>

My aunt, the late Sue Lane of Statesboro, was famous for this delicious casserole. It's a great side dish at holiday meals, but also makes a super Sunday night supper. A Savannah caterer used to serve it as an appetizer; she'd spoon it from a chafing dish to top a cracker.

6 tablespoons butter, divided	1/2 teaspoon prepared mustard, such
1 small onion, chopped	as Dijon
1 green pepper, chopped	2 tablespoons lemon juice
3 tablespoons flour	Salt and pepper to taste
1 1/2 cups whole milk, or half-and-half	1 pound crab meat, picked through
2 slices bread, toasted and	twice for shells
finely crumbled	1 cup soft bread crumbs
1 teaspoon ketchup	Paprika

Preheat oven to 350 degrees F. Sauté onion and green pepper in 2 tablespoons butter until tender.

In separate pan, make a white sauce. Melt 2 tablespoons butter, whisk in flour, and add milk or half-and-half, stirring until smooth and thick. Add toasted bread crumbs, vegetables, ketchup, mustard, and lemon juice to white sauce. Taste and season. Fold crab meat into white sauce mixture. Place crab mixture into 1 1/2-quart casserole, lightly greased.

In a small skillet, melt final 2 tablespoons butter; stir in bread crumbs until moistened. Top casserole with buttered crumbs. Sprinkle with paprika. Cover and refrigerate.

When ready to eat, preheat oven to 350 degrees F. Allow casserole to sit out at room temperature for 30 minutes. Cook, uncovered for 20 minutes, until hot and bubbly.

Baked Ham   Serves 16 to 20

A baked ham is a great item to have on the buffet table. I start with a good-quality, name-brand ham, cook it the day before, slice it, and store the slices in plastic freezer bags before the day of the buffet.

5- to 8-pound picnic ham, shoulder in	1 tablespoon prepared mustard or
1 cup brown sugar	2 to 3 tablespoons pineapple juice

Preheat oven to 350 degrees F. Place ham in a large roasting pan and place in the lower third of the oven. Bake for about 30 minutes per pound. The final 30 minutes, glaze with a mixture of brown sugar, and mustard, or brown sugar and pineapple juice. Return to oven for 30 minutes.

•••

Hope's Mac and Cheese   Serves 25

Hope Shearouse and her husband Steve run boys' and girls' homes in Mexico. This is her famous recipe.

3 cups uncooked macaroni	4 cups whole milk
1 tablespoon salt	1 pound sharp Cheddar cheese,
1 (8-ounce) jar of Cheeze Whiz	shredded
1/4 cup (1/2 stick) butter	1 pound Mozzarella cheese, shredded
5 eggs	

Cook macaroni in large pot of boiling water seasoned with salt. When tender, drain and return macaroni to pot. Add Cheeze Whiz and butter and stir. Combine eggs and milk in a medium bowl and whisk until blended. In the bottom of a 9 x 15-inch baking dish, place 1/2 pound of Cheddar and 1/2 pound of Mozzarella. Spread the macaroni evenly over the cheeses. Pour the egg-milk mixture over the macaroni. Stir together with a spatula. Pat down evenly in casserole. Top with the remaining Cheddar and Mozzarella. Cover and refrigerate.

   When ready to bake, preheat oven to 350 degrees F. Remove cover and bake casserole for 50 minutes to 1 hour, until center is set and cheese is lightly browned and bubbly.

Zucchini Bread   Makes 2 loaves

The flavor of this bread is a real surprise to most people who try it for the first time: It's sweet and spicy, like coffee cake. Savannah cook Jane Wells often gives the bread for Christmas. Her comment: "It's really a spring recipe, but I don't pare the zucchini and so there are green specks throughout and it looks Christmasy."

3 eggs	2 teaspoons baking soda
2 cups sugar	1 tablespoon cinnamon
1 cup vegetable oil	2 cups zucchini, grated (do not pare)
2 cups all-purpose flour	1 cup chopped pecans
1 teaspoon salt	2 teaspoons vanilla extract
1/4 teaspoon baking powder	

Thoroughly mix eggs, sugar, and oil in a large mixing bowl. Measure flour, then sift with salt, baking powder, baking soda, and cinnamon. Combine flour mixture with egg mixture. Add zucchini and pecans. Flavor with vanilla. Stir well.

Preheat oven to 350 degrees F. Pour batter into 2 greased-and-floured loaf pans, or 1 large Bundt pan. The batter will half fill the 2 loaf pans, or half fill the Bundt pan. Bake for 50 minutes for loaf pans or 60 minutes for Bundt pan. Bread should pull away from the sides of the pan, and a toothpick inserted in center should come out clean. Slice prior to buffet and store in a plastic container with snap-on lid.

Loaves freeze well.

Greek Salad   Serves 6 to 8

I wonder how many times I've made this in the 30 years since Pauline Georges, a great Greek cook, gave me the recipe. Maybe 100 times? At least! When I asked Pauline about the secret of her delicious Greek salad, she summed it up in two words: lemon juice. I have never altered her recipe, and I think of her every time I serve this dish. I often double the dressing recipe so I'll have some on hand in the refrigerator for salad emergencies.

1 small head of Romaine, or 2 Romaine
   hearts, washed and chopped
2 green onions, chopped in 1/4-inch
   pieces
2 stalks celery, chopped in 1/4-inch
   pieces
1 cucumber, with seeds scooped out
   and chopped into 1/4-inch pieces
1 large fresh tomato, chopped
   in 1/2-inch pieces
1 green pepper, cut in thin strips
2 ounces feta cheese, crumbled

1 dozen Calamata olives (large Greek
   olives with pits) or,
   1 can large black pitted olives

Dressing:
1/2 cup olive oil
1/4 cup vegetable oil
1/3 cup fresh lemon juice (about 3 lemons)
1 teaspoon salt
1/4 teaspoon freshly ground black pepper
1 clove garlic, minced or pressed
3/4 teaspoon dried oregano
1/4 teaspoon sugar

Prepare each item and store in a separate plastic bag. When ready to serve, place all of the salad ingredients in a very large salad bowl and toss. Pour about half of the dressing over the salad, toss and taste. Add more dressing if needed.

To make the dressing, measure all of the ingredients into a jar with tight-fitting lid. Shake until the dressing emulsifies. Store in refrigerator. Allow to come to room temperature before using.
  Makes 1 cup.
  Note: I said I had not altered the recipe, and that's not true. If you are serving this at a large buffet, you may want to go with black olives, which are not authentic, but are safer for those unfamiliar with Calamata olives, which have a hard pit. Also, you have to remove the pits from your mouth and dispose of them, which is not always the best scenario at an office party.

Toffee Trifle Bowl Serves 16-20

This is a great dessert because it feeds a crowd. It's brown, so save a little fresh whipped cream for contrast. Bernice Watson of Savannah shared this recipe with the bridge girls.

1 (5 3/8-ounce) package French vanilla
   pudding mix

3 cups half-and-half

1 pound angle food cake, torn into
   1 1/2-inch pieces

3/4 cup Kahlua

2 tablespoons instant coffee

2 tablespoons sugar

1 teaspoon vanilla

1/2 pound English Toffee, coarsely
   crushed, plus 1/2 cup for garnish

2 cups (1 pint) whipping cream, plus
   1 cup additional for garnish

Prepare pudding according to package directions, using half-and-half instead of milk. In large mixing bowl, sprinkle the cake with Kahlua and let stand for 5 minutes. Mix the pudding with the cake, and set aside.

Pour the whipping cream and coffee into a medium mixing bowl. Let stand 1 minute. Beat until thickened. Add sugar and vanilla. Beat until stiff peaks form.

In a 2-quart glass bowl or trifle bowl, layer the cake/pudding mixture with whipping cream mixture and crushed toffee. Repeat layers 2 or 3 times, ending with whipping cream and toffee for garnish.

When ready to serve, have a bowl of plain whipped cream to dollop on each serving, and additional toffee to garnish.

Christmas
Dinner

The season between Thanksgiving and Christmas is simply called "the holidays" and what it means is dragging out the best china, crystal, and silver that you own and serving the best dishes you can manage. So what if you don't have china, crystal, and silver and can't cook? Well, one of my friends had a lovely Thanksgiving meal on dinnerware that she had purchased from a discount store (she bought 32 plates for $2 a piece!), used palm fronds for placemats, and had dozens of candles for decorations. Please don't tell, but she went and picked up the turkey and dressing from a grocery store (She had preordered the meal; don't think you can just show up.) and had her friends each bring an assigned dish. Everyone had a lovely time.

Crispy Cheese Wafers

Here's the point: You can have a memorable holiday meal without making yourself crazy. Pick and choose from these recipes, or assign them all out to friends and family. You need to enjoy the day as much as anyone else. And don't forget when you're assigning, it's perfectly OK to ask for help in the kitchen, both before and after the meal. I have only one request: Please don't use paper plates. I'm OK with them for almost any other occasion, but not this one when you are showing your guests how much you care.

First, clean out your refrigerator and freezer of all non-essentials. This needs to happen in the week prior to the holiday cooking. Five days in advance, prepare the broccoli and sweet potato casseroles, the cranberry salad, the cheese wafers and the caramel cake and freeze them. Three days before Thanksgiving, begin to thaw the turkey in the refrigerator if you are using a frozen turkey. Two days before the holiday, chop every vegetable mentioned in the recipes and place them in labeled plastic bags and put them in the vegetable bin. Bake the rolls and place them in freezer bags and freeze. Make the crab stew. One day before, remove the casseroles and cake from the freezer. Do not remove the cranberry salad, as it remains frozen until an hour before serving. Make the cornbread for the dressing, bake the sweet potatoes and make the rolls. The night before Thanksgiving, mix up all of the casseroles. Remove the rolls from the freezer. Prepare the turkey for baking. Thanksgiving morning, get up early and put the turkey on. Remove all casseroles from the fridge an hour before baking so they won't be stone cold. Reheat the rolls and crab stew. Bake the pies while you are waiting on the casseroles to come to room temperature. Enjoy the smells and aromas—these are THE HOLIDAYS!

Christmas Punch Serves 8 to 10

Have all of the ingredients out on a sideboard with the recipe and have someone take care of this for you while you finish cooking.

2 cups orange juice

3 cups bottled lemon juice

2 cups pineapple juice

1/2 cup maraschino cherry juice

1 liter of Sprite

1 bottle of champagne

Simple Syrup:

2 cups sugar

1 cup water

Boil sugar and water 5 minutes. Refrigerate. Use syrup as needed to sweeten punch. When ready to serve, combine juices in a large pitcher. Taste for sweetness. Add simple syrup, if desired. When ready to serve, pour a little Sprite or champagne into a glass and pour the juice mixture over.

Crispy Cheese Wafers Makes about 4 dozen

1 cup (2 sticks) butter, softened

2 cups extra sharp Cheddar Cheese, grated

2 cups all-purpose flour

1/4 teaspoon salt

1/4 teaspoon cayenne pepper

2 cups Rice Krispies cereal

1/2 cup finely chopped pecans

Preheat oven to 350 degrees F. Combine butter and cheese in mixer. Sift flour, salt, and red pepper. Blend into butter/cheese mixture with stiff spatula. The mixture will be crumbly. Stir in cereal and nuts. Roll dough into small balls the size of marbles; the heat from your hand will help the dough hold together. Flatten with a small fork on ungreased, non-stick cookie sheets.

Bake for 11 to 12 minutes, or until lightly browned. Store in tins. Wafers freeze well.

Crab Stew Serves 12

Elizabeth Terry, chef of Elizabeth on 37th Street restaurant in Savannah, gave me this recipe for my first cookbook. I prepare this at least once during the holidays.

---

6 tablespoons butter

1 cup green onion, roughly cut

1/2 cup celery, roughly chopped

1 (2-inch) piece of carrot

6 tablespoons flour

2 1/2 cups milk

2 1/2 cups chicken broth, preferably
  homemade

1/4 teaspoon nutmeg

1/4 teaspoon white pepper

1/8 teaspoon cayenne pepper

1 cup cream

1/4 cup sherry

1 pound claw crab meat, picked
  through for shells

Melt butter over low heat in saucepan. Mince green onion, celery, and carrot in food processor. Or, mince by hand. Add vegetables to butter and cover saucepan with lid. Sauté over low heat for 5 minutes. Whisk in flour and cook for 2 minutes to remove starchy taste. Whisk in milk and broth. Bring to a boil, whisking occasionally. Add seasonings, cream, sherry, and crab.

Refrigerate in an airtight container. Reheat over very low temperature until very hot.

Frozen Cranberry Salad Serves 12

This is absolutely gorgeous. You unmold it directly from the freezer, then the cranberry layer begins to drip over the white cream cheese layer as it sits, causing a very fetching effect.

1 (16-ounce) can cranberry sauce,
  whole berry
Juice of 1 lemon
1 cup whipping cream, whipped
1/4 cup mayonnaise

1/2 cup confectioners' sugar
1 (3-ounce) package cream cheese,
  softened
1 cup pecans, chopped (optional)

Combine cranberry sauce and lemon juice. Pour into 3 1/2-cup mold sprayed with vegetable spray or into a square dish. Combine whipped cream, mayonnaise, sugar, cream cheese, and pecans, if using. Spread this over cranberry layer. Freeze. Cut into squares or unmold onto a cake plate.

Roast Turkey with Gravy   Serves 12

Everyone has their "first turkey" story. Mine is cooking the giblets in their plastic bag inside the turkey, and discovering this only upon carving the bird at the table as everyone looked on!

1 (12- to 14-pound) turkey	2 tablespoons flour
Salt and pepper	2 cups turkey broth
2 tablespoons butter	Salt and pepper, as needed

If turkey is frozen, defrost in refrigerator according to package directions. When thawed, rinse turkey inside and out in cold water, being sure to remove remove giblets and any plastic bags stored in the cavities. Dry with paper towels. Season inside and out with salt and pepper rather heavily.

Preheat oven to 325 degrees. Place turkey breast side up on roasting rack. Roast turkey in the lower third of the oven, uncovered, according to package directions, typically for 3 to 3 ½ hours for a 14- to16-pound bird, until juices run clear and drumstick wiggles freely. You may need to make a loose tent of aluminum foil and place over the bird for the last hour of cooking to make sure the drumsticks do not overbrown.

Remove turkey. Allow it to sit for about 30 minutes before asking someone to carve it for you. It is much nicer to have all of the meat on a serving platter than to try to do this during the meal.

To make gravy: Take a whisk to loosen all pan drippings in bottom of roaster. Strain into a glass measuring cup and add water to make 2 cups. In a medium saucepan, melt butter. Stir in flour and whisk until this is blended. Slowly add turkey drippings. Stir until thickened and heated. Season to taste with salt and pepper. Can be refrigerated and reheated. Makes 2 cups.

•••

Cornbread Dressing   Serves 12

3/4 cup butter or margarine	2 teaspoons salt
1 cup chopped celery	1 1/2 teaspoons pepper
1/4 cup finely chopped onion	1 1/2 teaspoons poultry seasoning
4 pieces of toast, finely crumbled	3 cups chicken broth
5 cups cornbread, finely crumbled	4 eggs, beaten

Melt butter in heavy skillet. Sauté celery and onion. Put crumbled toast and cornbread in large bowl. Pour butter and vegetables over. Add seasonings. (I refrigerate this in a plastic bag and add the eggs and broth Thanksgiving morning). Add eggs and broth. Stir well. Place in a 2-quart casserole, sprayed with vegetable spray.

Preheat oven to 350 degrees F. Bake uncovered for about an hour, until set. Serve with turkey gravy.

Alternate Holiday Menu

Believe or not, some people are tired of turkey by Christmas. So, this menu is for my beef lovers—standing rib roast and cheesy potatoes are hard to beat. The casseroles go with either menu as accompaniments.

Standing Rib Roast   Serves 12

A rib roast is very costly, so it is best to buy one when they go on sale and have a butcher remove all of the meat around the eye, and shorten the bones. When you are ready to roast, the guide, according to the late Julia Child, is 12 to 13 minutes per pound for rare; 14 to 16 minutes for medium rare, and 17 to 20 minutes per pound for medium (so our 5-rib roast would cook for 2 ¼ to 2 3/4 hours.) You must allow at least 30 minutes for the roast to rest after cooking.

1 (5-rib) roast, trimmed	**Horseradish Sauce:**
2 teaspoons salt	1 cup mayonnaise
1/2 teaspoon pepper	1/2 cup sour cream
1 teaspoon garlic powder	2 teaspoons prepared horseradish

Rinse the outside of the roast and pat dry. Place the roast in a roasting pan. Combine the salt, pepper, and garlic powder. Rub this mixture over the roast.

Preheat the oven to 325 degrees F. Cook the roast until it is 120 degrees F for rare, 125 degrees F for medium rare, and 140 degrees F for medium, about 2 1/4 to 2 3/4 hours. (Smaller roasts will take less time). Allow roast to sit on the counter at least 30 minutes prior to carving. Lay the roast bone-side down and carve thin slices of beef. Serve with horseradish sauce.

To make the horseradish sauce: Combine ingredients in a small bowl with snap-on lid and stir well. Taste. Add more horseradish if desired. Makes 1 1/2 cups.

Delmonico Potatoes Serves 6-8

6 medium white potatoes, peeled and
  cubed
10 tablespoons butter or margarine,
  divided
6 tablespoons flour

2 cups half-and-half
Salt and pepper to taste
10 ounces sharp Cheddar cheese,
  grated
1 cup soft bread crumbs

Boil potatoes in a 2-quart saucepan in water to cover, until fork-tender. Drain well and place in shallow 2-quart baking dish. Make white sauce by melting 6 tablespoons butter. Whisk in flour; add half-and-half and whisk until smooth. Season with salt and pepper.

Pour white sauce over potatoes. Cover casserole with grated cheese. In small saucepan, melt remaining 4 tablespoons butter and add bread crumbs, tossing to coat well. Sprinkle bread crumbs over top of cheese. Cover with plastic wrap and refrigerate until ready to bake.

When ready to bake, preheat oven to 350 degrees F. Remove plastic wrap. Bake casserole for 30 minutes or until cheese is melted and casserole is bubbly.

Scalloped Oysters Serves 8 to 10

1 pint shucked oysters, washed and
  drained well
2 cups oyster cracker crumbs
1/4 cup melted butter
1/2 teaspoon salt

1/2 teaspoon pepper
1 cup half-and-half
2 teaspoons sherry
Dash Tabasco
1 teaspoon Worcestershire sauce

Preheat oven to 400 degrees F. Mix cracker crumbs and butter. Arrange a layer of half the buttered crumbs in 1-quart baking dish. Layer oysters over crackers. Season with salt and pepper. Cover with remaining crumbs. Combine half-and-half, sherry (if using), tabasco, and Worcestershire. Pour over casserole. Bake for about 20 minutes, or until liquid has been absorbed.

Sweet Potato Souffle Serves 10 to 12

Is this a side dish or a dessert? Who cares? It's delicious and beautiful. It would also be a wonderful accompaniment to the wild game supper.

4 cups sweet potatoes, mashed
  (approximately 2 large potatoes)

2 eggs

1 cup sugar

1/4 cup (1/2 stick) butter or margarine,
  melted

1 teaspoon vanilla

1 tablespoon orange juice

Topping:

1 cup brown sugar

1/2 cup flour

1 cup chopped pecans

1/2 cup (1 stick) butter, melted

To bake sweet potatoes, wash and dry and puncture skin several times with a sharp paring knife. Place the sweet potatoes on a baking sheet and bake for 45 minutes to an hour at 350 until they are very tender when pressed with your fingers. Peel away the skin and remove strings from the potatoes. Place them in a large deep mixing bowl. Combine sweet potatoes, eggs, sugar, melted butter, vanilla, and orange juice. Spread this into a greased 3-quart casserole dish.

Preheat oven to 350 degrees F. Combine topping ingredients in a small mixing bowl. Stir with a fork. Crumble over potatoes. Cook casserole for 30 minutes, until brown and bubbly.

Spinach Souffle   Serves 8

I grew up eating frozen spinach souffle, and was determined to create a comparable recipe. This casserole dish is always wiped clean at my holiday dinners, so I think it's a winner.

1 (10-ounce) package frozen chopped spinach
1/2 cup finely minced onion
1 tablespoon butter
3 additional tablespoons butter
3 tablespoons all-purpose flour
1/2 teaspoon salt
Pinch of cayenne
1/2 teaspoon ground black pepper

1 cup half-and-half
1 1/2 cups grated Swiss cheese
1/2 cup grated Parmesan cheese
4 eggs, beaten well

Preheat oven to 325 degrees F.

Cook spinach in a small amount of boiling water for about 5 minutes, or cook on high in the microwave in a glass dish for 2 minutes. Allow to cool, then squeeze out all of the liquid. Place spinach in a medium-size mixing bowl.

Sauté onion in 1 tablespoon butter until soft. Add onion to spinach.

In the sauté pan, melt remaining 3 tablespoon butter. Whisk in flour, salt, and pepper and slowly add half-and-half, continuing to cook until mixture thickens, 3-5 minutes. Turn off heat. Stir in the Swiss cheese and Parmesan and continue stirring until mixture is smooth. Pour sauce over spinach in mixing bowl. Add beaten eggs and stir well.

Pour spinach mixture into a round, 2 1/2–quart casserole that has been sprayed with vegetable spray. Place casserole in larger pan filled with 1 inch of water (this will give the casserole a smooth texture.)

Bake for 45 minutes. Serve immediately. Souffle will puff up, then deflate, but will still be delicious!

Cloverleaf Rolls   Makes 2 ½ to 3 dozen rolls

Of course you can buy rolls from a bakery or from the frozen food section of your supermarket. But if you can make your own, it will put you on the culinary map. These can be baked several days prior to the meal, refrigerated, and reheated just before serving.

1 cup boiling water	3 envelopes yeast
1 cup (2 sticks) butter, cut into chunks	1 cup warm water
1/2 cup sugar, plus 1 additional teaspoon	2 eggs, beaten
2 teaspoons salt	7 cups bread flour

Pour boiling water over butter in large mixing bowl. Add sugar and salt and stir until sugar is dissolved. In separate bowl, combine warm water, yeast, and 1 teaspoon sugar. Allow yeast to foam, about 10 minutes. Pour yeast mixture into butter mixture. Add eggs. Blend well.

Add flour, one cup at a time, until soft dough has formed. A heavy-duty mixer with dough hook is excellent for this. If using mixer, knead dough until smooth and elastic, about 5 minutes. Or, knead by hand about 10 minutes, until dough is smooth and elastic.

Place dough in greased bowl and turn to coat all sides. Cover with clean tea towel. Allow to rise until doubled in size, about an hour. Punch dough down. Pinch off small pieces of dough and roll into balls about the size of marbles. Place 3 balls in each cup of a large muffin tin that has been sprayed with vegetable cooking spray. Cover loosely and allow to rise until doubled in size, about 1 hour.

Preheat oven to 325 degrees F. Bake rolls until lightly browned, about 20 minutes. Allow to cool completely on wire racks, then transfer to freezer bag and keep refrigerated. When ready to serve, reheat at 275 degrees F for about 5 minutes.

Rolls may also be frozen.

Caramel Cream Cake Serves 16

I am going to let you in on a little secret: I have made this recipe with a boxed cake mix! Prepare according to package directions and divide the batter evenly among 3 8-inch round or square cake pans.

Cake Layers:

1 cup (2 sticks) butter

3 cups granulated sugar

6 eggs

2 2/3 cups all-purpose flour

1/4 teaspoon baking soda

1 teaspoon salt

1 (8-ounce) carton sour cream

1 tablespoon vanilla extract

Caramel Frosting:

1/2 cup (1 stick) butter

1 cup light brown sugar

1/4 cup evaporated milk

1/2 teaspoon vanilla extract

2 cups confectioners' sugar, sifted

6 to 8 toasted whole pecans, for garnish

Have all ingredients at room temperature. Preheat oven to 350 degrees F. Spray 3-inch or 8-inch round or square cake pans with vegetable cooking spray and dust them with flour.

Cream butter until light and fluffy. Add sugar and continue to beat until very light. Add eggs, one at a time and beat well after each addition. Sift flour, baking soda, and salt. Add about 3/4 of the flour mixture, then a little sour cream and combine thoroughly. Repeat, alternating flour and sour cream, beginning and ending with flour. Stir in vanilla. Pour batter into prepared pans. Tap pans on counter top several times to remove air bubbles. Bake for 20 to 25 minutes, until cake tester comes out clean. Do not overbake. Cake will pull away from sides of pan when done. Remove from oven onto cake racks when done. Cool 10 minutes. Remove carefully from pan.

Frost between layers with Caramel Frosting. When cake is assembled, frost top and sides. Decorate with toasted whole pecans.

To make the frosting: Melt butter and add brown sugar. Cook 2 minutes over medium heat, stirring constantly. Add milk and bring the mixture back to a boil. Turn off heat. Add confectioner's sugar and vanilla. Beat with a wooden spoon until the frosting is smooth. Let cool slightly. Frost while frosting is still warm. If it hardens, reheat over very low heat.

To toast pecans: Place pecans on baking sheet. Toast in toaster oven on lowest setting for about 3 minutes. Decorate cake with toasted pecans.

Cake freezes well.

Chocolate Chip Pecan Pie   Serves 8

There are a number of variations of this recipe, and it goes by many names. It is my favorite hurry-up special-occasion pie. It's absolutely delicious hot, with ice cream. But I also like it chilled, when the texture changes from fudge-like to chunky.

1 cup sugar

1/2 cup self-rising flour

1/2 cup (1 stick) butter, melted
  and slightly cooled

2 eggs, slightly beaten

1 1/4 cups chopped pecans

1 1/4 cups semi-sweet chocolate chips

1 (9-inch) deep-dish pie crust, thawed,
  and unbaked

Whipped cream

Preheat oven to 350 degrees F. In a medium mixing bowl, stir together the sugar and flour. Add other filling ingredients, stir, and pour into pie crust. Bake for 50 minutes to 1 hour, until filling is set.

Let cool for 10 minutes before serving. Garnish with a dollop of whipped cream.

Also excellent served cold.

New Year's
Buffet

Here's the thing: If you are in the South on New Year's Day, you simply must eat a meal that includes greens to ensure good cash flow and cow peas or black-eyed peas to bring good luck in the coming year. Serving a pork tenderloin oozing with bleu cheese and cheesy corn bread just makes good sense—the pork is for prosperity, and the cornbread is to sop up all of the delicious "pot likker" in the bottom of the greens pot.

This meal goes particularly well when polished off with pecan pie, truffle cake, or red velvet cake.

Now, you can start the New Year off right by serving this at the stroke of midnight, right after the ball drops and you smooch your favorite person, or you can save it for New Year's Day lunch. Whichever direction you take, prepare the greens (turnips or collards from the Gullah meal), rice, and Hoppin' John the day before. Put the pork tenderloin and corn bread in the oven 45 minutes before you are serving dinner. You'll feel lucky to have such a delicious way to usher in the New Year.

Pork Tenderloin Stuffed with Bleu Cheese   Serves 6 to 8

1 pork tenderloin

4 ounces bleu cheese

2 ounces cream cheese

1 tablespoon fresh thyme; leaves
    stripped and finely chopped

1/4 teaspoon salt

1/4 teaspoon ground ginger

1/4 teaspoon garlic powder

1/8 teaspoon ground pepper

2 tablespoons vermouth

Preheat oven to 400 degrees F. Allow cream cheese to become very soft at room temperature, or heat in microwave for 10 seconds. Combine with bleu cheese and fresh thyme. Trim ends of tenderloin if necessary to make tenderloin uniform. Separate the two tenderloin pieces and evenly distribute the cheese on the larger portion. Cover with the smaller portion and tie the two together with kitchen twine.

Combine salt, ginger, garlic salt, and pepper in small bowl. Rub mixture over outside of tenderloin, covering all meat. Place in glass baking dish. Bake uncovered for 30 minutes. Meat thermometer should register 140 degrees F. Remove tenderloin to serving platter and allow to stand for 10 minutes before cutting.

Whisk vermouth into pan juices in baking dish. Spoon a teaspoon or so of this over each piece of sliced pork, if desired.

Cheesy Corn Bread   Serves 6

1 1/4 cups stone-ground corn meal

1 cup cream-style corn

1 cup sour cream

1/3 cup vegetable oil

1 tablespoon sugar

2 eggs

1/4 teaspoon salt

2 teaspoons baking powder

1 cup shredded Cheddar cheese

Combine all ingredients, stirring by hand. Pour into well-greased 8-inch square pan or round cake pan. Bake at 400 degrees F for 40 minutes, until well-browned. Allow to stand 10 minutes before cutting.

Hoppin' John   Serves 6 to 8

I used to cook the rice and peas together, but discovered I really like the peas and their juices served over hot rice. Be sure to serve with pepper vinegar, a Southern requirement. This is the dish that will being you luck in the New Year.

1 1/2 cups dried cow peas, or
    black-eyed peas, soaked overnight
1 cup celery, chopped
2 medium onions, chopped
1 medium green pepper, chopped
2 small ham hocks, or a large meaty
    ham bone

Salt and pepper to taste
1 cup rice, approximately
1/4 cup minced onion
1/4 cup minced green pepper

Drain off soaking water. Cover peas with fresh water and cook peas with celery, onion, green pepper, and ham hock in a heavy bottomed pot with a lid until peas are done, about 2 1/2 to 3 hours. Continue to add small amounts of water if peas appear too dry. Remove ham hock or bone, pick meat from bone and return to pot if desired.

   Prepare rice separately, according to package directions. Serve peas with juice over rice; garnish with a sprinkling of minced onion and green pepper if desired.

   You can prepare this in advance and reheat in a microwave.

Chocolate Truffle Cake Serves 12

16 ounces semisweet chocolate,
  broken into small pieces
2 1/4 cups granulated sugar
1 1/2 cups (3 sticks) butter, cut up
1 scant tablespoon granular instant
  coffee
1/2 cup boiling water
9 large eggs
Cocoa powder

Whipped Cream:
2 cups whipping cream
1/3 cup confectioners' sugar
3/4 teaspoon vanilla
2 tablespoons cognac or rum

Raspberries for garnish, optional

Place oven rack one-third up from the bottom of the oven. Preheat oven to 250 degrees F. Butter the bottom and sides of a 10-inch springform pan. Line bottom of pan with a paper liner. Butter paper. Dust pan and paper with unsweetened cocoa powder. Invert pan and tap to remove excess cocoa.

In a heavy 3-quart saucepan over low heat, melt chocolate, sugar, and butter. Dissolve coffee in water and add to mixture. Stir until very smooth. Turn off heat and allow to cool slightly.

In a large bowl, beat eggs with wire whisk. Gradually add slightly warm chocolate mixture, beating constantly with whisk until very smooth. Pour mixture into prepared pan. Place on a baking sheet and place in oven. Bake for 2 hours. (Some of the batter may run out of the springform pan during baking.)

Turn off oven, open door slightly and let cake stand for 30 minutes. (It will fall slightly in the middle.) Remove from oven and allow to cool completely at room temperature. Remove sides of pan and refrigerate cake while it is still on the bottom of the springform. When completely cool, you can invert the cake onto a cookie sheet, remove the paper liner from the bottom of the cake, then turn it quickly back on a decorative plate for serving. Or you can wrap the cake tightly in plastic wrap and freeze. Thaw completely before serving. Serve narrow wedges with whipped cream.

To make the whipped cream: Whip all ingredients together in a chilled bowl until stiff. Serve large dollop of cream on top of a wedge of chocolate truffle cake. Dust top with unsweetened cocoa. May garnish with ripe raspberries if desired.

Red Velvet Cake   Serves 16 to 20

This cake is always appreciated at holidays. The deep red color comes from the food coloring and the cocoa powder.

2 1/2 cups all-purpose flour

1 1/2 cups sugar

1 teaspoon baking soda

1 teaspoon salt

1 tablespoon cocoa powder

1 1/2 cups vegetable oil

1 cup buttermilk, room temperature

2 large eggs, room temperature

1 ounce red food coloring, about
   1 1/2 tablespoons

1 teaspoon white vinegar

1 teaspoon vanilla extract

Cream Cheese Frosting:

2 (8-ounce) packages cream cheese,
   at room temperature

1 cup (2 sticks) butter, at room
   temperature

4 cups powdered sugar, sifted

1 teaspoon vanilla extract

1 cup pecans, finely chopped

Preheat the oven to 350 degrees F. Spray 3 (9-inch) cake pans with vegetable cooking spray, then add about 1 tablespoon of flour and tap the pans until all of the surfaces are covered with flour. Sift together the dry ingredients, and place them in the bowl of an electric mixer. Whisk together the oil, buttermilk, eggs, food coloring, vinegar, and vanilla. Add the liquids to the dry ingredients and mix well, scraping down the bowl several times.

Divide the batter evenly among the cake pans. Place the pans in the oven—two will fit on one rack and the third on the lower rack. Rotate half-way through cooking. Bake for 25 to 28 minutes, until the edges pull away from the sides of the pan and a toothpick inserted in the center of the cake comes out clean. Do not overbake.

Place the pans on the counter. Run a knife around the edges. Use a plate to remove the cakes, then re-invert them onto a wire rack to cool, rounded-side up. Cool for at least 15 minutes.

To make the frosting: Combine the cream cheese and butter and mix well. Add sugar slowly and mix again. Add vanilla and mix. Stir in pecans.

To frost the cake, place 1 layer, bottom-size up, on the cake plate. Use a spreader to spread icing to within an inch of the cake. Top with another layer, bottom-size up, and spread this with icing in the same way. Top with the last layer, rounded side up, and frost the top and sides of the cake.

Index